HOME FREE

Ann Guilfoyle

"A very helpful, nicely organized guide." *Booklist*

As a working woman, parent and grandparent, Ann Guilfoyle has had to keep the home fires burning with a minimum of stress. Here she passes the secrets along, covering order, cleaning tools, techniques, laundry, food shopping and storage. Running through the book are tricks for establishing a less-work household, sharing jobs, and modifying habits to reduce housekeeping time.

Home
Free

ANN GUILFOYLE

The No-Nonsense Guide
To House Care

John Curley & Associates, Inc.
South Yarmouth, Ma.

Library of Congress Cataloging in Publication Data

Guilfoyle, Ann. Allen County Public Library
  Home free.   Ft. Wayne, Indiana

  Bibliography: p.
  1. Home economics.   2. Time allocation.
I. Title.
TX147.G84 1985   640   84–20018
ISBN 0–89340–880–8 (lg. print)

Published in Large Print by arrangement with W. W.
Norton & Company in the U.S.A. and Henry Morrison,
Inc, for the U.K. and Commonwealth.

Distributed in the U.K. and Commonwealth by Magna
Print Books.

Printed in Great Britain

THIS ONE'S FOR YOU, MA!

Contents

Home Free

Author's Note

The less-work tactics offered in these pages are for those people who have little time to give to homecare. For the sake of simplicity, I have made many value judgments; these are based on 20-odd years of balancing the demands of self, family, career, and home. Although my natural aptitude for domesticity is nonexistent and my inclination for self-improvement minimal, experience has convinced me that ignoring housework causes more problems than it solves. In other words, I have come to terms. My home environment may never qualify as perfect, but it works well enough for me and for those with whom I share it. *Home Free* passes along my methods as well as the results of research during the writing of this book. All recommendations are time efficient, simple, *and* effective, the three criteria for inclusion in this book. Cutting down on time alone was not good enough. Results had to be worth the effort!

The days when household skills were learned at mother's knee seem to be long gone, so many elementary procedures – such as how to wield a broom – are covered. Such procedures along with much of the cleaning information are meant to impart the basics. The reader might want to skim these sections initially, referring to the index for specific information. Other chapters contain more generalized solutions to common household problems, abstracted from the experience of busy, other-directed homemakers. Since every household is as individual as the people who create it, your own solutions may be somewhat different, but this information will point the way.

There is further need for information pooling. Modern homemakers are bucking long-standing precedents established when homecare was more or less a full-time occupation. We are being forced to adapt practically overnight to new conditions and new ways. I would enjoy hearing from readers who have evolved their own time-efficient methods. Please send letters to me c/o my publisher, W. W. Norton & Company, 500 Fifth Avenue, New York, N.Y. 10110.

Product brand names are used throughout the book. In most cases, these are simply examples of the type of product that should be used. In some instances, product recommendations *are* offered. These are the result of personal experience, based on conditions and surfaces in my home. My own standards of excellence also come into play. They may not be the same as yours. It's best to proceed with care whenever you use a new product – or technique. Read product labels, follow directions, and always keep an eye out for adverse effects.

Many people have contributed to the content of this book. I've not set foot in a friend's house in the past three years without asking questions about homecare. No one seemed to mind, and many of the answers have found their way into these pages. Special thanks are due to Vivien and Jon Zegel, whose homestyle has served as my "less-work" model. While managing to put in less housecare time than any other team I know, they consistently maintain a comfortably used, showplace of a home. The Zegels stand as proof positive that it can be done.

Veronica Hornby helped greatly with the research and kept me supplied with a steady stream of pertinent books. Michelle Epstein shared her interest in the subject matter and her clipping file. Mary Norton Boyce, who is a professional cleaner, generously donated practical know-how. Julie Guibord Rozin read chapters for relevance and supplied us with the drawings that appear on page 205. Special thanks are due Regina Rector, Christina Stark, Glenna Kophen, and Bob Gravini (New York State College of Human Ecology/Cornell University), and Martin Gellman, director of the New York City Bureau of Food Affairs. Carol Houck Smith, my editor, made many contributions. I am particularly grateful to her for the book's title, which I find inspired.

Personal thanks are in order to Skip Rozin who gently coached along an amateur writer. And to Leo Banks, my partner, who worked to implement every household experiment and who countered every angst-provoked "I can't do this!" with a simple "Of course you can."

ANN GUILFOYLE

One

The Goal: A Clean Comfortable Place In Half The Time

A house, any house, is filled with things that refuse to take care of themselves, that require regular nurturing and an occasional dose of intensive care. I, for one, would not fault anyone who chose to spend life in a handy motel room with daily maid service and a 24-hour eatery in the lobby. However, most of us opt for more conventional roots and in so doing take on a fair share of household responsibility.

Once, not so long ago, there was another way out. It took some early planning and a bit of luck, but if you could manage to be born male, you were reasonably assured of avoiding all but the most casual brush with housework. No more. We live in hectic times and all hands are needed on all fronts. Men as well as women are expected to pitch in.

A lucky few are able to afford regular help, but even they are not "home free." Today's

5

hired hands, useful though they may be, rarely do it all. More often than not, they are part-timers who are not available to shop for food, prepare meals, wash dishes, or attend to the day-to-day picking up and light cleaning that ensures a comfortable household.

Take my word for it, there's no way out. Housework is here to stay and the more you know about its essential skills, the less of it you will have to do, the quicker the jobs will be finished, and the happier you will be with your living space. In time, you may actually come to feel that the effort expended is energy well spent. The essential goal, after all, is not to care for things but to enhance life. People feel more sane in an orderly environment. They are also more comfortable and sometimes even more happy. Think of the arts and crafts of homemaking as part of your survival kit; they serve best when used to create a small island of safety in what can be a pretty rough world.

Nobody does housework the way it used to be done, not even your mother. Ideas have changed, work-saving tools have been invented, and the fabrics, paints, and finishes we live with have toughened up. The work requirements are not as stringent as they used to be. Besides, there is less available time today than there was even a few years ago. Our energies are needed elsewhere and when we finally make it home, there are better things to do than clean. Unfortunately, modern technology has yet to produce a house that will run itself. The only insurance of home comfort is a firm human hand. The problem, always, is to manage to get the jobs done and still have enough of *you* left over to enjoy the results. It becomes a question of balance – and of choice.

Two

The Compromise Principle

The first principle of less-work homecare is expedient compromise. Stop trying to do it all. It's not necessary. If you're struggling to fit housework in between the cracks of a too hectic life, it may not even be possible.

Set sensible standards based on the needs of your household and the amount of time available. When standards are too high, homemaking becomes an irksome responsibility. There's always something more to be done and you are rarely satisfied with what you can actually accomplish. A hidden streak of perfectionism is often an underlying cause of an apparent inability to cope. Jobs are put off until tomorrow, so they can be done "right." Tomorrow proves to be a long time coming. Meantime, jobs multiply and problems compound. Sooner, not later, the home environment falls apart.

Establish priorities and devise basic routines. Be sure that meals are adequate and that fresh clothes and bed linens are available.

Keep the kitchen clean and bathroom tidy. Pick up well enough so that living spaces and work areas are reasonably serene. Give special attention to valued possessions such as the white couch, your shiny wood floor or Persian rug. When fundamental systems function smoothly, people are comfortable and able to go about their daily concerns. If time is short, attend to basic routines and consider the rest optional; fit it in as best you can, when you can, *if* you can.

Schedule the jobs that are necessary to essential operations. Most household chores, when promptly done on a regular basis, are easily attended to. Let them go too long and digging out becomes a problem. When there's no way to schedule a regular housework day, do things a bit at a time. Vacuum one evening, clean the bathroom another, the kitchen yet another. Shop for food one night a week on your way home from work. Do the laundry on the weekend. Tackle big tasks the same way. Straightening every closet in the house can take a whole day; one closet, especially one that has not had an opportunity to get out of hand, will take no more than 15 minutes. The important thing is not to let jobs pile up or get so big that getting them done requires more time (or interest) than you've got to give.

Once basics are attended to, concentrate on the things that show. Any household can pass muster if clutter is contained and if horizontal surfaces are kept clean and show-off possessions polished. Attending to visible systems is a fair compromise that can be the end-all and be-all of your housework if you are willing to coexist with the underlying, if nonapparent, confusions that result.

Practice cosmetic strategies that fool the eye. Keep up the white chair and everyone will assume that the black one is equally clean. Wax the tabletop and no one will notice the legs underneath. When company's coming and things aren't up to par, bring out the candles, dim the lights, and serve up good food and conversation. After all, no one really cares. As long as soil or disorder doesn't force itself on the attention, no normal person will seek it out.

Make practical work-saving choices when you decorate or purchase clothing. These selections need not be dreary. A less-work life-style can still be attractive, even luxurious if that is your bent. But whenever you buy anything, in addition to considerations of fit, affordability, and appropriateness, ask yourself, "Will this save me time?" If you feel you must have the white shag rug no matter what, then by all means buy it, but be prepared to give it the time it needs. Every household deserves a few such extravagances, but the space (or closet) they occupy takes a lot more effort to keep up.

If you possibly can, hire help. A cleaning person who comes in once a week, or even twice a month, makes a world of difference. If you can't afford this easiest alternative, be creative. Neighbors, schoolchildren, and college students are all possible sources of assistance who might be able to take over one or two jobs, such as laundry, food shopping, and dishwashing, for considerably less than it costs to hire a professional.

Enlist the full cooperation of everyone who shares your space, including children. Housework becomes a senseless burden when it's constantly being undone. Establish firm pick-up, put-back rules and insist that others clean up after themselves, especially in the kitchen and bathroom. When there's no full-time homemaker, the work must be shared, or the one responsible for it all will experience burn-out. Two children over the age of eight equal one full hand; two adults working together can do the work in less than half the time. If your people won't cooperate, or for some reason can't, consider whether your standards are too high. Sometimes when expectations are lowered, it's easier to get the other guys to help out.

Achieve better, longer-lasting results by doing jobs the right way. The skills of housework are so easily learned and so simple that to do them correctly takes about as much effort as a half-hearted attempt. Have good tools on hand and an adequate selection of cleaning agents. The proper materials, artfully applied, can reduce your time and work drastically. A housework regime is a lot like an exercise program. The hardest part is getting started. Once you become proficient, there's a lot less resistance to doing it.

A TROUBLE-SPOTTING ASSESSMENT QUIZ

Everyone seems to feel some embarrassment when the quality of housekeeping is mentioned, even those who appear to be doing a perfectly fine job. There's obviously some kind of mass neurosis, enforced by the false impression of home life presented by the media. (Have you ever seen a pile of dirty dishes or an unmade bed on a situation comedy?) Home-styles have changed, but the old feelings and guilts linger. The quiz that follows is designed to help you rise above outdated mores and pinpoint the actual trouble spots in your home operation. It zeroes in on the basics, the systems that provide the comforts and necessities that help you along in life, and leaves the degree of neat and clean up to you. Give your psyche a break and take the quiz in a healthy spirit of self-interest. The point is to determine what wants doing to bring your home as close as possible to the way *you* want it.

Base your answers on conditions as they are right now. Ignore the questions that do not apply to your life. They will not affect the final result.

1. When conditions are normal, your house can be surface cleaned and laundry done:
   A. Easily, in less than four or five hours.
   B. With some effort, but in no more than five or six hours.
   C. With great difficulty in eight hours, with a few jobs left for another time.

2. To prepare a meal, you would:
   A. Begin preparation immediately. The kitchen is in working order.
   B. Centralize a few used dishes, put away a few odds and ends, and wipe off the counters.
   C. Need first to wash dishes, pots,

utensils, and eating implements and scrub at least a corner of the counter space before you felt it safe to cook. *Or* settle for a peanut butter sandwich.

3. To put your sleeping area into apple pie order, it would be necessary for you to:
   A. Do nothing.
   B. Pick up a few items of clothing and make the bed.
   C. Change the linens and put away a significant accumulation of clothing and assorted miscellany.

4. You and other members of the household:
   A. Have an adequate supply of clean clothing and a change of sheets and towels.
   B. Are OK (barring emergencies) until next wash day, which normally arrives before everything gets dirty.
   C. Have been down to rock bottom for more than two days.

5. If the mailman were to knock on the door and express an urgent need to use the toilet facilities, there would be:
   A. Nothing in your bathroom that you

would be embarrassed for a stranger to see.

B. A moment of hesitation, followed by a more or less confident "Be my guest."

C. A short delay, while you put things in order.

6. If you were to take a piece count of items in your communal living areas that are *conspicuously* out of place (including dirty dishes, mail, clothing, and reading matter), for each person using the space you would find an average of:

A. Two items or less.

B. Four items or less.

C. Five items or more.

7. A reasonably intelligent houseguest who needed to use such items as a hair dryer, ruler, or can opener, could find them:*

A. Easily without much of a search.

B. With a bit of effort, but in fairly short order.

C. With great effort and possibly not at all.

*Note: Good organization is always built on logic that is usually readily discernible even to a stranger.

8. Normally, your refrigerator and pantry contain:
   A. Makings for several nutritious main meals as well as lunches and breakfasts.
   B. Makings for a few nutritious main meals as well as lunches and breakfasts, but some supplies are low.
   C. Almost nothing with which to prepare a proper meal of any kind.

9. If a neighbor drops by to discuss community affairs, you:
   A. Invite him or her in with no hesitation.
   B. Make casual apologies before inviting in because things are a bit out of order.
   C. Talk in the doorway, holding the door closed behind you, because you do not want anyone to see the mess inside.

10. Imagining that circumstances have forced you to neglect household operations for some time, to bring the house back to tip-toe shape would take:
    A. A long day of relatively concentrated work.
    B. Two days of hard work.

C. More than two days of all-out effort. *And* you discover that a few things cannot be restored to peak condition. The fabric on the couch is worn and permanently discolored. A large stain on the rug won't come up. Several patches of the no-wax kitchen flooring have lost their shine and are obviously scratched.

Scoring

A is the "ideal." B represents a working compromise; although somewhat less than optimum, the system functions well enough for all normal purposes. C means that the area under examination is out of your control. Too many C answers obviously add up to trouble. To determine your overall home-style, tally up your A, B, and C answers.

Majority A: An A status is only worthwhile when it comes easily. Most Type A's spend too much time and effort doing too many things too well. If you're feeling the strain, give yourself a break. Relax your standards and learn to compromise.

Although it's not really necessary, it is possible to establish an easily maintained, time-efficient A household. This is most easily done when home surfaces are resistant to soil, when partners and/or children carry a full share of responsibility, when cleaning skills are correctly applied, when proper tools are used, and when a cleaning person comes in once a week.

Majority B: For most of us, B is the sensible place to rest. A high B score means that home systems are pretty much in place and functioning. Housecare may not be perfect, but it's good enough. However, if you are a low B bordering on C, you would do well to modify your operation before the next crisis hits. Every chapter in this book contains hints for streamlining the home operation. Put as many as possible into practical use, and *read the next few paragraphs.*

Majority C: Before you go any further, ask yourself, "What are my current circumstances?" If things are chaotic because you have been too distracted to attend to the house, then you no doubt know what to do when the pressure eases off. Once you've restored order, try to improve the homespace so it is easier to maintain (see Chapter 3) and establish an emergency routine to see you through when there's no time (see Chapter 11.)

If you live with others, the difficulty may be that you have not yet established a collective approach to housework (see

Chapter 4). When one person is too busy, the others should be able to keep things afloat. Even when everyone is overloaded, if each person manages to assume a part of the responsibility, things will not get completely out of hand.

The chronic Type C is another matter. Firm steps must be taken to ensure that basic home needs are met. Some organization is called for, as well as a commitment to a certain routine, no matter what. Follow the sympathetic guidelines in Chapter 11 and remember, nothing good comes easy.

Three

Creating A
Less-work Household

CARE-LESS DECORATING

There are many finishes, colors, and materials that retain their freshness, that are not hurt by neglect, or that clean so easily that maintenance is a minor responsibility. The more of these you include in your home, the less work you have to do. It's that simple. There are plenty of readily available less-work choices that can be made, enough, in fact, to accommodate any taste. Because few of us start from scratch, but already have our homes in place, modifications are usually done one by one. Try to include at least one major improvement a year, budgeting time and money to get it done. Never do a big job, such as painting a wall, without incorporating a less-work measure as outlined in this section.

When you make decorating decisions bear in mind that floors, carpets, and upholstered furniture can be badly damaged if not regularly maintained. Those who tend to be more erratic about housework should choose finishes and fabrics that are soil resistant. Walls can sometimes be washed and can always be repainted, but both of these are big disrupting jobs that are best avoided or postponed. Homes that house young children are always at risk. Simply picking up after them is work enough; don't compound the effort by having fragile or hard-to-clean surfaces and furnishings.

Choosing Colors

Use whites and pastels with caution. Light colors make a space seem larger and more open and airy, but they also are quick to show soil. To achieve the effect with less aggravation, select easy-to-clean soil-resistant fabrics and surfaces.

Use dark colors with discretion. A chocolate brown rug that sees a lot of traffic, or a navy couch visited regularly by a fair-haired cat, may have to be vacuumed daily if you want to keep it looking its best. *But* soil and stains won't show! Many people choose dark colors because it is easier to vacuum than to wash. A dark wall can go much longer without being repainted. Catch-22: Dark colors make a space seem smaller (and darker). Those who spend daylight hours at home usually prefer lighter colored walls. At night, however, the use of spotlights can create the illusion of size. Lit areas are bright and cozy while those that are unlit seem to disappear, which can make even a closet-sized room appear much larger than it is.

Medium tones blend in with dirt and are a possible balance between light and dark. Walls painted in such tones, or floors carpeted in them, tend to fade into the background making walls or floors unobtrusive, even in the daytime. The result is a sense of expanded size.

Muted colors, such as beige or mauve, show soil less than bright vibrant colors, such as yellow or pink. A bottle green is a better choice than kelly green, steel blue is preferable to royal, and rust works better than orange. Use bright colors as accents or where they will stay clean.

Some patterns, tweeds, and textures camouflage soil beautifully, making it possible to work light colors into an expedient decorating scheme. Those patterns that utilize only light colors are less satisfactory than those that combine light and dark. A tweed couch or carpet that mixes brown and beige gives a light effect while remaining fresher longer. A patterned wallpaper with lots of white in it gives almost as much feeling of space as an all white wall but doesn't show every fingerprint. Nubby textures that create some shadow help to disguise soil on fabric and carpeting. Rough textures used on walls, such as barn siding or stucco, rarely if ever need to be cleaned as long as they are not too near a kitchen. A brick wall, even one painted with white enamel, can go for years with no more attention than an occasional flick of a feather duster.

Upholstered Furniture

Imagine what your hair would look like if you shampooed and rinsed it with a damp sponge. That's often how upholstery fabric is cleaned. And if you apply enough water to clean the fabric properly, you'll damage the padding underneath. Natural fabrics, including the soft rough cottons and heavy canvases frequently offered in white, are troublesome to maintain. Soft cottons absorb soil and wear out quickly; canvas retains dirt with such a vengeance that it must be cleaned with hot water and a scrub brush; even then, the results are problematic. Velour must be dry-cleaned, and dry-cleaning methods are even less satisfactory than wet methods. A washable blend of natural and synthetic fibers, or all synthetic, is your best bet. A

Scotchgard or similar treatment can help to postpone cleaning. If the fabric is not already treated when you purchase it, have the merchant arrange for it to be done before the furniture is delivered. Products containing a Scotchgard-type treatment are available for home application, but it is best done professionally through a cleaning service. Such finishes must be renewed from time to time. No matter what the fabric or the finish, choose colors with care. In the end, they are your best protection.

A few upholstery fabrics hold up well even after long, hard use. Chintz, for instance, is naturally stain resistant, often comes in busy patterns (good for camouflage), and stays attractive even when faded. Nonpastel cut or antiqued velvets hold up well, are easily damp cleaned (although deep cleaning calls for a dry process), and their texture helps to disguise effects of wear. The same is true of needlepoint and dark-colored brocades.

While the all-cloth look is attractive, it's not the most practical. A few alternatives: leatherlike vinyl is practically trouble free and can look and feel remarkably like leather. A hard-surfaced leather is also moderately easy to maintain. If you choose a chair or couch that sits on a wood base, the base can easily include hidden storage compartments;

home-oriented magazines often give directions for building such furniture. These designs, as well as those that have wooden backs and sides on which the cushions rest, are relatively carefree; cushions can be re-covered when the fabric has passed its prime or when you want to change your color scheme. One friend created a new look without sewing a stitch. Cloth, cut to fit, was folded carefully around each cushion and secured with a big safety pin. When cleaning time arrived, covers were easily removed and tossed into the washing machine. A pre-shrunk heavy cotton is a good fabric choice that tends to fade nicely with repeated washings.

Carpeting

Think twice before installing wall-to-wall carpeting. While it is certainly good looking, many find it hard to care for. Anything that is permanently installed must be cleaned in place and any such method is less than satisfactory. Also, heavy traffic areas are quick to show signs of abuse, causing overall appearance to suffer. A large room-sized rug, which can be cut from carpeting, is a fair compromise. It can be shifted around from time to time, and sent out to a professional cleaner who can sometimes redye stained or discolored spots. Padding under a rug helps to prolong its lifespan.

Olefin, the least expensive of the commonly used carpet fibers, holds up well under neglect and cleans beautifully. It is, however, more likely to crush than other fibers and should be chosen in a low-level weave. Nylon is the strongest fiber, but it generates static electricity that attracts dust and soil. The newer nylons, such as Antron and Enkalure, have more built-in static control and soil resistance than older ones. Polyesters and acrylics are fairly soil resistant. Wool only serves well if it is first quality.

Carpeting can be chemically treated to make it more resistant to soil and static. This is better done by a professional carpet cleaner, although products are available in houseware shops should you want to treat the carpeting yourself.

Texture and color should also be considered when selecting a carpet. Shags and multilevel piles are hard to maintain. Weaves that feature short, solidly packed loops or twists survive nicely in heavy traffic areas and vacuum easily. Tweeds or patterns show less soil and lint than solid colors. Oriental-style rugs in darker colors are good, but these can fade surprisingly quickly where exposed to bright sunlight. Industrial flat-weave carpets are enjoying a bit of a vogue in the home. Some of these serve well; others show traffic patterns and stains. Here, it seems to be a matter of getting what you pay for.

Flooring

Wood floors require frequent attention with a vacuum or broom and periodic applications of paste wax (a *big* job). Those protected by polyurethane, a rough-tough, less-work finish, are a snap to maintain, although care should be taken to protect the surface from wear. If polyurethane varnish wears away in a heavy traffic area, the whole floor must be refinished. High-gloss finishes highlight dust and scratches; satin finishes are more tolerant of neglect.

No-wax resilient vinyl floor coverings are attractive and simple to keep up, but must be swept often to protect the shiny surface; eventually, these surfaces lose their gleam. Light- or bright-colored coverings show soil and scratches; dark colors show footprints. Solid colors are more troublesome than patterns.

Furniture

Wood is easily maintained, especially if it

is not waxed too often. Oiled finishes require less work than wax. Pieces that receive heavy use, such as desks or tabletops, do well with a barlike finish (see page 302). Plastic laminates are susceptible to scratches, stains, and burn marks but, with a little caution, are among the most easily maintained furniture surfaces. Glass and chrome show dust and fingerprints but wash like a charm. Glass is impervious to everything except breaking; some, but not much, care must be taken to prevent scratching chrome. Clear plastics, such as Plexiglas, scratch and burn too easily and are damaged by alcohol, making them unsuitable for tabletop use.

Walls

Flat paint absorbs soil and is difficult, sometimes impossible, to wash clean. Many professional cleaners refuse to have flat-painted walls in their homes. Semiglossy and glossy oil-based paints are more resistant and almost always come clean with comparatively little effort, but they call attention to surface imperfections. A vinyl-coated wall covering hides many faults and is easily kept up. As mentioned earlier, rough-textured surfaces, such as barn siding or brick, rarely show soil, although they must be dusted occasionally. These surfaces are usually absorbent, however, and almost impossible to wash. They are best kept away from kitchens, or anyplace else where they are exposed to grease. Smooth-surfaced wood paneling, or plastic laminate, is simply maintained as long as you do not wax it.

When dealing with walls, remember that not all walls receive the same degree of wear. One vulnerable wall camouflaged by paint or paper or covered with a resistant material can help an entire room to retain its good looks. Always paint baseboards and doors in enamel (semigloss is fine) and consider using a darker color, especially for baseboards.

CONTROLLING THE THINGS OF HOME

The normal household contains more than 3,500 items, yet most of us actually use fewer than 15 percent of those possessions on a regular basis. The rest, even though they may come in handy now and then, spend most of their time gathering dust and getting in the way. The household items we use most often are essential life tools. When they are accessible and ready to go, the home stage is set for productive activity. Pleasures come easy, confusion is held to a minimum, and work is done quickly with little waste motion when key possessions are stored conveniently in a fashion that implements their use. With this kind of commonsense order, life support systems fall into place and comfort follows.

When dealing with systems in which many things are kept and used in one space, organization is crucial. The pay-offs are greatest in the kitchen, the bathroom, and where clothing and linens are stored.

To establish order, weed out the nonessentials. Eliminate those things that do not further your comfort or survival. Too many possessions are kept simply because they are there. A few items that many have chosen to live without: table linens, hand towels, books that are never read, outdated clothing. *If* you don't need an item or want it, throw it out or give it away. A proven fact: Anything that hasn't been used for two years will almost certainly never be used. In the process of cutting down, don't be too hard on yourself. Those old ballet slippers that symbolize a long ago dream may be just as important to your good life as an extra pair of sheets (although the sheets *are* entitled to better storage space). If you are a "collector" and find yourself with more decorative objects than you have time to care for, start a favorite-thing exchange with yourself. Display a few and store the rest to be pulled out and exchanged with the regulars when your home spirits need a perk.

Go through the house periodically to eliminate items you no longer want. One possible criterion: When you barely "notice" a decorative object, it may be time to dispose of it or consign it to deep storage. Similarly, when you consistently pass over a tool or article of apparel in favor of another.

Beware of multiplication. Every time we turn around there are new things taking up space and demanding attention. Don't be too quick to take in new ones. Some people live with a trade-off system. Whenever something new is added to the household inventory, something old is discarded.

Remove as much as you can from your field of activity. Keep rarely used items in out-of-the-way spots on high shelves and at the back of closets. If you're short of space, be innovative. Department stores sell storage boxes made to fit under a bed. Corners, which are usually wasted space, can easily accommodate a new closet or handy cut-to-fit shelves. Some householders lower the ceiling of an entryway or small room and use the space above the false ceiling as an "attic." If you simply don't have room at home, consider renting an outside storage locker.

Decide which of your possessions are most essential to your day-to-day operations and give them accessible permanent locations close to where they will be used. A bath towel, for instance, should hang next to the shower or tub. When mail is always opened at the breakfast table, this is the spot for the letter opener, not on the desk in the study. If a special storage container, hook, or shelf will make a thing more accessible, provide one. Do all you can to further a smooth traffic flow. If the drawer sticks, fix it. If there's something else in the way, move it. Try not to stack or crowd a primary object. Best space is that which is the most easy to reach. This space is always at a premium; reserve it for those things that deserve it. Give them hanging space or arm-level shelves or drawers; keep them on the counter or bureau top or in the forefront of the cupboard. Give your next best space to useful objects that are needed less frequently. Put these behind or under primary objects; stack them or keep them in front of your high or low shelves.

Base storage decisions on *real* function, determined by use, rather than the name or shape of an object. Try to keep items together that are used together. Keep the salad bowl near the chopping block and store the punch bowl on the highest shelf or in the back of the coat closet, along with the holiday decorations. An evening shirt does not rate the same prime space ʼs those shirts worn to business. Besides, if you keep such an item in the traffic mainstream, it will probably have to be pressed before its next wearing.

A Place for Every, Everything in Its Place

The vast majority of our possessions are movable objects like clothing, dishes, books, and such mundane objects as ball-point pens. In other words, most of them are things that are easy to pick up and put down again *in the wrong place*. To avoid this, set up some general rules for placement and stick to them. Putting an object back where it belongs is always the job of the person who used it last. When rules fail, investigate the situation and the cause for lapses. Sometimes an aid to neatness, such as a more accessible coatrack or a well-placed laundry hamper, is needed.

Use common sense to think recurrent problems through in creative ways. Objects that are used in more than one area are most likely to be mislaid. One expert suggests that the place where a thing turns up most often is probably where it belongs. Sometimes it makes sense to own more than one of an item that is much in demand. An extra pair of scissors kept handy to where you read the newspaper will allow you to clip items of interest on a regular basis, and help to ensure that the paper shears remain at the desk.

To forestall the confusion that occurs when objects are not kept in an orderly fashion, it's wise to devise storage systems appropriate to your needs. There are many easily installed storage aids that make home organization simpler and more efficient; and new products seem to come on the market every month.

Clip-on and stackable drawers and sliding wire or plastic baskets come in a wide range of sizes that can be utilized anywhere to modify or expand existing facilities. Some of the stackable designs stand on wheels, allowing for *portable* storage, which can be especially useful in a child's room or when doing the laundry. Lightweight wire hanging shelf systems made to slip over the back of a door can turn it into an extra cupboard with narrow shelves. Often used to provide a cook with more pantry space, these versatile systems can also accommodate hobby supplies, an assortment of small tools, or underwear and clothing accessories. Lazy Susans, designed to hold small containers on a kitchen shelf or counter top, are equally useful for grooming sundries on a dressing table. Art supply shops offer Lazy Susans with compartments designed to hold the miscellany of a commercial artist. These can also be used in the home to keep objects like pencils, pens, scissors, paper clips, and postage stamps in one place. Others might consider putting such a turntable to use on a bathroom counter for storage of toothbrushes, combs, cosmetics, and so forth.

It's the rare clothing closet that provides adequate hanging space. Most clothing (jackets, blouses, shirts) is half-length, which means that the space between the bottom of the garment and the floor is wasted in a conventional closet. a split-level arrangement in which rods are hung at the top of the closet and at it's center, with one smaller rod placed high on one side to accommodate longer garments, practically doubles the usable space. A do-it-yourselfer can create such a system easily, but there are also ready-made devices that adapt to fit any size closet. For those with wide closets, see-through plastic drawers or wire shelves are also useful. A row of these running up one side of a closet is much more convenient than hard-to-reach shelves at the top.

Out-of-the-way storage for rarely used items is somewhat easier to achieve than work-a-day placement of those possessions that are in frequent demand. The more limited your space, the more difficult it becomes, but solutions to spatial problems need not be complex. In fact, the simpler the better is a good rule to follow. One clever adaptation was devised by a woman living in a one-room apartment. She kept about 12 wicker suitcases (the kind sold by Oriental import shops and usually used as picnic baskets) stacked decoratively against one wall. Each container held items related to *one* particular interest or activity (such as correspondence, travel mementos, snapshots of friends and family, and needlework accessories). She kept one basket empty, ready for once-a-year projects such as Christmas cards or papers for tax returns. Each basket was inconspicuously labeled on its side so it could be removed from the stack and carried to her desk or easy chair when an activity was in progress. To keep order, it was only necessary to return the items to their basket and close it. Even when several activities were going on at the same time, the room looked fine.

A favorite solution of those who are short of space is a low, flat chest, which can double as a coffee table or bench-type seat. These can present a problem, however, because objects stored inside must be stacked one upon the other, and such storage arrangements tend to lose their order. To help keep the contents both neat and accessible, see-through plastic boxes can be used for various categories of possessions. Another solution when space is at a premium is to cover one or two occasional tables with a floor-length cloth. There's a goodly amount of storage potential underneath.

There are other practical and ingenious solutions to the space problem. Some people hang their bicycles on their entryway walls, where they are out of the mainstream yet easily reached. I've heard of one couple who keep a canoe suspended from the ceiling of a New York City apartment. A recent newspaper article showed the living room of a woman who collected antique clothing. All garments that were not being worn were simply hung on the wall as part of the decorating scheme. The same clipping shows a wardrobe of hats displayed in a similar fashion. Resourcefulness is often put to the test in tight quarters.

Making Order Work

Many people resist reordering their existing structure because, imperfect though it may be, it functions – more or less. The idea of disrupting a working system to create a new order is particularly disturbing to a householder who has too little time. To make it easier, don't plan to do everything at once; do only what you can finish in a finite period. An extra half hour on laundry day is often enough time to impart new sense to a linen closet or bureau drawers. A kitchen utility drawer can be attended to in the time it takes a dishwasher to complete its cycle. The allocation of a few extra hours when you shift from summer to winter garb may be all it takes to reorganize your clothes closets. Incorporate a small amount of reordering into every week's routine, and soon you will rack up a significant accomplishment.

Be prepared to give some jobs more time. It took me a full weekend to establish a new system in my kitchen – after several weeks of preparatory thought! *But* after two years, the new order is still in place; the kitchen is so functional that I unconsciously cooperate with the system by returning things to their proper place. An effective storage system is so closely aligned to patterns of use that it is actually easier to utilize it than to ignore it. Should you find yourself resisting a new system, take it as a clue that further refinement is necessary.

The bathroom medicine chest and auxiliary storage facilities offer an easy opportunity to perfect organizational techniques. This confined area, which can usually be put in workable shape in a few hours, amply demonstrates the most common obstacles to easy order – too much variety, too many things, too little space.

To begin, spread a sheet on the floor and empty the contents of the medicine chest and any related storage areas onto it. Include any things you normally keep at the sink or side of the tub. Group objects together that share a common purpose, for example, first aid supplies, medicines, hair grooming aids, tools for oral hygiene. Discard anything that can be disposed of and ask yourself as you work, "Does this *really* belong here?" If you always manicure your nails while watching TV in the bedroom, then manicure equipment belongs in a bedroom drawer, not in the bathroom. Perhaps you have a guest lavoratory in which the medicine chest is going to waste. This could serve to hold medicines and first aid supplies. I use my extra bathroom as a makeup room.

Free as much space as you can and turn your attention to items used on a daily basis. Assign these permanent places that will implement their usefulness. For instance, if you dry your hair at the bathroom mirror, a wall hook or counter stand placed near the mirror will hold the drier most conveniently while saving needed shelf space. A decorative jar kept nearby on sink or countertop might contain styling brush and comb and other hair-related aids. Shampoo and conditioner are usually best relegated to the shower area; a hanging shelf that slips over the shower head can be purchased at any houseware shop.

Think through all your daily bathroom activities in a similar fashion. Give high shelves to infrequently used medicines or sundries such as suntan lotion. If possible, keep bulky items and reserve supplies in the cabinet under the sink. You may discover that no matter what you do, there is not enough existing storage space to house your bathroom inventory. Easily installed cabinets and shelves that match a bathroom decor can be found at any sizable houseware or bathroom specialty shop, along with a handsome assortment of storage aids such as toothbrush holders, makeup organizers, and childproof lock boxes for medicines.

When creating any system, consider your own temperament. For those who are happy with loose structure, a tightly ordered environment may mean too much monitoring, in which case failure is inevitable. A more flexible approach might be better. In my kitchen, for instance, I have a large rack of hooks running along the wall between the stove and sink. The half near the stove accommodates pot holders and an assortment of frequently used pots. The half nearest the sink belongs to colander, sieve, vegetable steamer, teapot, and apron. For obvious reasons, the only items that have a precise (never-to-be-changed) location are the pot holders. All other hooks are on a first-come, first-served basis within the allocated half of the rack. When I first reordered the kitchen, I tried assigning a specific hook to each item; it made me crazy! I'm perfectly content with this more casual set up even if it sometimes takes me a few extra seconds to place my hands on a tool. One tip: in a loose system, a clear visual field is necessary to find what you want quickly. Don't crowd a loosely ordered space with too many items.

A person who requires tight order for emotional comfort would do well to attempt to modify that need. Modern life rarely allows time or energy for total perfection around the house. This person will also do well to lighten the load by cutting back severely on possessions. The Japanese have known for centuries that the perfect ordering of not too many things is not only attainable but an excellent way to provide a restful, aesthetic environment.

When establishing order is beyond you, get help. Consult a friend who has the knack or get a good book on the subject. *Getting Organized* by Stephanie Winston is a commonsense classic in the field.

Closing thought: Order and perfection are not synonyms. All that's ever needed is good enough.

PREVENTIVE MEASURES

With a bit of anticipation and foresight, you can maintain a comfortable household with less work in less time. Many of the following tips are freely borrowed from the old-style housewife and have been passed down from generation to generation.

Keep dirt and mud from being tracked in by stopping them at the door. A *pair* of rough-textured mats, one on the outside, the other inside the entryway, is a good idea. Some households institute the practice of taking off shoes at the door and donning slippers. Even if you are not willing to make this a regular routine, don't allow wet foot gear beyond the entry. Winter is especially rough on floors. The chemicals used to melt ice and snow are death to wax and don't do much for a carpet, either. Absorbent throw rugs (with nonskid backings) placed in front of bathroom and kitchen sinks will also help to cut down on floor washing chores.

Prevent a conspicuous buildup of soil in areas of heaviest use. Turn room-sized rugs and area rugs several times a year so traffic is equally distributed; rotate cushions on couches and chairs. Use small rugs to protect waxed floors and carpets where they are subject to extraordinary use, such as the dining area and the social nook, usually defined by couch, coffee table, and comfortable chairs. Machine-washable bathroom carpeting comes in a wide range of decorator colors. The largest size (five by eight feet) covers a generous space. Consider inexpensive, see-through plastic floor runners for heavily used passageways or investigate the expensive moppable rubber matting, which is sold by the yard and is available in bright colors as well as neutrals; look for simple embossed designs that change the institutional appearance to one of "high tech."

Slipcovers keep upholstery clean, but they are expensive to have custom-made and ready-mades rarely come in the size you need. Well-placed decorative throws draped over favorite roosting spots are an attractive alternative. A knitted afghan, a woven blanket, or even a section of washable lace (perhaps cut from a tablecloth) can be used to good effect. Some practical souls simply tuck over-sized terry towels around their sofa or seat cushions. When colors match that of upholstery, these are not especially obtrusive and they can be quickly removed when company comes.

Use decorative receptacles to help keep clutter under control. Have one bowl or basket to temporarily house small objects that have no current home. When the receptacle overflows, give things a place of their own or dispose of them. Assign convenient permanent spots for small restless items that would otherwise end up on the tabletop (or be mislaid). A hook attached near the door will keep keys handy and out of the way. A small jar on the bureau top might hold change or earrings.

If messy housemates are your problem, toss their out-of-place belongings into a big cardboard box. When asked where you put the "what-not," indicate the box. Have a laundry hamper in each bedroom. A two-hamper system, one for machine washables and another for dry-cleaning and hand laundry is most helpful. Keep a waste basket in each room to encourage prompt trash disposal.

Work out an easy bed-making system. The most popular approach is to use fitted bottom sheets and substitute a quilt for a spread so that the "made" bed can be easily assembled in the morning; patterns and dark colors disguise stains and wrinkles are less obtrusive. Some people eliminate top sheets entirely and use a soft quilt that can be thrown into the washing machine along with the bottom sheet. Those who dislike blends of cotton and polyester might investigate the new no-iron cottons, which feel better next to the skin.

Eliminate as much airborne soil as you can. You might hang sheer curtains at the windows and keep them drawn, especially when windows are open. These effectively capture a lot of dust and are easily washed, which is more than can be said for walls, furniture, and Venetian blinds. An air conditioner is another good dust trap, as is a room-sized air purifier, but only when filters are kept clean. Even small air-cleaning machines have their place, and that's next to the favorite ashtray of a smoker. A hood over the stove will cut down on the spread of kitchen grease, a major component in hard-to-clean soil. The filtered hoods are fine when you have no means of providing an outside vent.

Put flat floor protectors on the feet of tables and chairs so they can be moved without scratching the floor finish. Keep movable furniture away from walls or paste felt strips on chair backs to protect wall surfaces from scrapes. Chair-level wooden wainscoting, installed on the walls around the dining table, is decorative and less likely to scratch than plaster walls.

Confine food consumption to specified areas. Supply coasters for drinks and small plates for snacks. Do not fill glasses or cups to the rim and avoid crumbly or drippy finger food when entertaining.

Establish the routine that children wash up when returning home from outside and *after* meals. Along the same vein, confine potential troublemakers – crayons, paints and clay – to a specified play area and don't allow markers into the house until youngsters are old enough to be responsible for them.

Modify children's rooms so that they can help to maintain them. Supply child-sized features, such as a bed that's easy to reach, a low dresser with nonstick drawers, a closet with hangers and hooks at a child's height. Include a great big wastebasket, a laundry hamper, and a catch-all for toys. All fabric items such as throw rugs and bedspreads should be machine washable, in colors that are dark enough to hide mishaps like spilled paint. Walls are best covered with an easily washed substance, such as vinyl wall covering or glossy paint.

A few tips for pet owners: Commercial nylon doormats are good catchers of paw dirt. No rubbing is necessary. Get the largest possible doormat and if you don't like the appearance, take it up when you entertain. Keep a towel handy near the door to dry the dog after a walk in the rain. Keep the dog's coat (and your walls) clean with frequent baths. A dog, encouraged to overcome its fear of vacuum noise, actually enjoys being vacuumed. Mine follows me around on cleaning day waiting for his turn at the hose. Cats, at least my cats, will not accept the vacuum. Brush them instead.

Four

Help!
Working Together
And Hired Hands

When it comes to housecare, the more willing hands the better. The home in which everyone contributes a full, fair share of work is easily maintained with no great sacrifice of time or effort from any one individual. When one person is temporarily unable to help out, the others know what to do to keep it going. The cooperative attitude actively reduces home tensions while it helps to forge a sense of cohesiveness and shared purpose.

Two adults working together can clean a house, cook a meal, or organize a closet in considerably *less* than half the time it takes one person working alone. Professional cleaning services that send out teams instead of individual workers take advantage of this. Each team member is assigned an area of responsibility that utilizes similar skills and tools. This system allows each worker to develop judgment and to perfect techniques.

When assignments are made, physical attributes are taken into account. The strongest worker does the jobs that require muscle; a taller one gets those in which height or a wider arm span makes a difference.

When working with another, never take your partner's performance for granted. Carry on loudly and at length about an extraordinary job, such as a perfectly polished table, and verbally acknowledge even ordinary efforts; encourage others to do the same. Few of us work simply for the sake of getting the job done. We need to know that our contribution is valued. When improvement is called for, point it out gently and be specific. "That table needs more work" will not improve matters half so much as "I see you missed a few spots with the polish. That table's in a dark corner. Do you think turning on the light would help?" The only time to come down hard is when someone is obviously shirking. And even here, light comments are usually more effective than loud complaints. When criticism is necessary, address the quality of the work, not the character faults of the person who's doing it. If matters don't improve, perhaps a redistribution of jobs is called for. You may be overestimating the ability, say, of a child or the task may be incompatible with the personality of the person doing it. A switch of jobs might be all that's needed.

Watch out for the "boss" syndrome. In the end, the boss is always responsible for everything. Responsibility for housework is a burden that is better shared. When you introduce someone to a new skill, take time to see that it's mastered. Work along with people to show how a job is done; give some idea of why it's being done and what problems may be anticipated. As soon as coworkers become proficient, back away and let them be responsible for results. As much as possible, try to allow group pressure to maintain the home standard. When something is not up to snuff, hold back and give the other guys a chance to gripe and possibly solve the problem.

THOUGHT FOR THE DAY

There are 168 hours in a week. If you spend 56 hours sleeping (8 hours 7 times a week); 48 hours on the job, going back and forth; 10 hours on your personal grooming; 10 hours eating meals; 10 hours loving, friending, perhaps parenting; 6 hours tending to irregular necessities (trips to the dentist, caring for sick kids, buying a new automobile, searching for the perfect bathing suit, overcoming temporary incapacitating depression), you will have 28 hours left in a week. *Twenty-eight hours.* This is the time that you have left for housecare. It is also the *only* time you have left for yourself.

Here's another schedule, just to give you something to think about. It is based on the "typical" weekly time requirements for running a household containing all the normal accoutrements. It does not include major tasks such as window washing, oven cleaning, or floor waxing.

	Hours	Minutes
Laundry (sorting, washing, drying, folding, putting away)	2	
Ironing		30
Mending		10
Food shopping; storing	2	
Meal preparation (breakfasts, dinners, take-along lunches)	7	
Vacuuming	1	
Cleaning a bathroom		15
Cleaning kitchen		45
Dusting, polishing, damp cleaning		30
Changing linens		10
Daily: washing dishes and straightening up kitchen	5	
Daily: Pick-up (straightening up, putting away accumulated clutter, quick sweep or dust if needed, 3 beds)	3	
TOTAL (GRAND) Author's comment: HA!	22	20

Be sure that you are not imposing too high a standard. When work is being honestly shared, all partners are entitled to a say in how well things have to be done. If you're the only one who wants jobs done better, reexamine your expectations and make adjustments. When you relax job standards for others, lower your own as well. If one person does too much things are likely to backfire. When exhaustion or resentment builds up, arguments ensue. Housework is never worth fighting about.

Children

Because children are shorter and have less strength than adults, they cannot do every job and what they can do takes longer. But even a preschooler, working along with an adult or older child, can help. Including the youngest may slow progress, but it is an essential first step in helping that child feel part of the home work force. At the same time that a cooperative spirit is encouraged, the youngster learns the basic skills. Little kids are willing helpers, ready to do far more than they are capable of. One common reason that older children are reluctant to assist is that too often initial eager attempts to please were brushed aside.

In general, a child over the age of eight can

accomplish about half as much housework as an adult, so long as the jobs are right for the youngster's strength, motor skills, and attention level. Washing an entire wall is too hard a task; cleaning an oven or washing windows high above ground level is too risky. Teach children to respect the cleaning agents they are using so they will not hurt themselves or cause damage (see page 236). And don't expect a youngster to put in a full day's work. A few hours is about all that can reasonably be expected of an eight-year-old. A 14-year-old can probably achieve as much as an adult, once safety rules are established and techniques are learned, but this depends on the responsibility level of your teenager. If yours is easily distracted or prone to daydream, don't give your child a potentially dangerous job.

When it comes to maintaining their rooms, younger children may need some assistance, but older ones can certainly be responsible for their own space. A few thoughts on the subject.

Once you've helped to create it, a child's room and the things in it belong to the child. If you take over too much responsibility, the child will feel the room belongs to you, *not* to him or her. Such feelings of nonownership have a lot to do with a later inability to maintain order. It's better to give children the instructions they'll need to take care of their own possessions and then to help out only when necessary.

You might spend a few pick-up minutes with young children each night and a bit more on cleaning day. Let it be part of your time together, a good time. As much as possible let the child do the work, while you sit back and carry on a conversation. Slip advice in between the news of the day. Don't get impatient and don't demand too much. Why not let him wear the wrinkled T-shirt that was balled up and tossed in a corner and decide for himself whether or not he cares to do it right next time? A mislaid toy may cause tears, but future toys will stand a better chance of being put back in the right place. As the child matures, this routine will die a natural death, along with the bedtime story. About then, the child is ready to take responsibility for his or her own space.

Ideally, the rooms of older children, particularly adolescents, should be off limits to adult interference. In response to a sincere request, you might help rescue a space that has fallen into total disarray or assist with big jobs, such as wall or window washing, that are too much for a child to do alone. Suggest systems – but better to wait until you're asked

– that will make it easier to keep up the space. A sense of order is always a private matter and establishing one that is individual is part of the maturing process. Systems imposed from above deprive a youngster of an opportunity to practice control or study the effects of a lack of it. Unless the room reaches a level of mess that threatens to infect the rest of the house, the best policy is hands-off. If the appearance bothers you, keep the door closed. When a room is shared by more than one child, act as moderator but try to be just. The child who cannot accept rigid order is no more of a villain than one who demands too much.

Your offspring should, of course, realize that they are expected to take an active part in the maintenance of community space. In doing this, the skills of housecare will be learned, so they can be applied when the children are ready to maintain their own space to a "higher" standard.

Woman's Work

The old chestnut that housework is woman's work is still with us. Some men won't do their share, no matter how you cajole or reason. When dealing with an untenable labor situation, the measure of last resort is to go on strike. This is a kill or cure tactic. Most of the time, the guilty party comes to see the error of his ways, or at least knuckles under, but sometimes the relationship is sundered, the striker replaced by more willing labor. If you're not ready to risk ending a relationship, don't try it. Instead, do everything you can do to reduce the workload. Read Chapter 1, and apply as much of its advice as possible. Pressure your partner to do some "man's work" and have him improve home surfaces so that care requirements are reduced. Apply the compromise principle strongly and do as little housework as you can while still keeping essential systems in place. After that, focus only on things that show (or which offer *you* comfort). Better yet, get your partner's agreement that more of the household income will go for hiring help. Sending out his shirts and having a cleaning person can take the place of the effort he's not willing to make.

Assigning the Jobs

When doling out household tasks, try to achieve a balance by assigning jobs that require a similar amount of effort and time. Obviously every home environment is individual, but the jobs grouped below are usually considered of equal weight.

Doing the laundry (including folding and putting away)
Shopping for food (including putting way)

Preparing dinner
Washing dishes; tidying up kitchen

Vacuuming floors and furniture
Light cleaning of kitchen and bathroom
Ironing; mending

Dusting; damp cleaning
Damp-mopping floors

Defrosting the refrigerator
Cleaning stove and oven
Waxing all the furniture
Washing all the windows
Washing picture glass; mirrors

Dumping trash baskets; taking out garbage
Light dusting; putting things in order
Light vacuuming or sweeping heavy traffic areas
Making bed; picking up bedroom
Errand running

When it comes to hired hands, what we get is largely determined by what we pay. When money's no object, it's possible to find someone who can handle all aspects of household responsibility including shopping for Christmas presents. Such ability can easily command a salary of $20,000 a year plus room and board and full insurance benefits! Most of us, when we're lucky, get along with a day worker who comes in once a week, or twice a month, to surface clean and perhaps do laundry. The ideal cleaning person takes pride in performance, has the required techniques down pat and can normally be counted on to put in an appearance when expected. Few find the ideal, but even someone who is not totally dedicated to the cause can ease the burden.

The surest way to obtain someone right for your needs is through a friend. Not just any friend, but one who has a home similar to your own and a comparable approach to housework. Household standards are individual, and so are the problems that different homes present to a cleaning person. To be effective, a hired hand needs to mesh with the style and expectations of the household. A casual cleaner who is masterful at "pick up" can be a godsend where clutter is the primary problem and cleaning a secondary concern. The neat-as-a-pin householder, however, does not want a pick-up service but expects excellent cleaning skills knowledgeably applied.

The Options

Cleaning services, which until recently were primarily used by offices and institutions, are beginning to dominate the home cleaning scene, especially in nonurban areas. A reliable service trains its staff so that each worker delivers good standard results. When any one cleaner is unable to come to work, the service simply substitutes another, a very important consideration for those of us who count on outside help to keep the house livable. The services carry insurance as well, which covers any damage done. Most services normally limit themselves to specified operations including vacuuming, dusting, spot cleaning, washing floors, and cleaning the bathroom and kitchen. They do not pick up, wash dishes, make beds, or do the wash. Usually, two people work together, and the job is done amazingly fast. Extra work, such as window washing or oven cleaning, is done by appointment only after an additional fee is negotiated. Larger organizations have the equipment and expertise to handle all heavy-cleaning operations including rug and furniture shampooing and floor waxing. Many small services are actually "mom-and-pop" operations. When this is the case, you may run into the same kind of problems that you would find with any independent operation (discussed below).

The old-style cleaning person, almost always a woman, generally takes a more personal approach to housework. They are often housewives earning money by doing what they know best. This independent worker pays attention to detail and tackles the smaller, time-consuming jobs, like straightening out a closet or doing laundry, that a service won't touch. Even a skillful cleaning person, however, may not be as good at big jobs as a service team. Some households combine both approaches, occasionally hiring a service for the more arduous chores while employing an independent cleaner for maintenance. The occasional day worker is sympathetic to the problems of the messy housekeeper and will dig in and handle things like a week's accumulation of dirty dishes. A few have mastered the problems of cleaning and can restore even neglected possessions to good shape. Many self-taught cleaners, however, are not adequately grounded in basic techniques, which can mean that prized possessions are damaged, and unless you have insurance to cover them, you're out of luck.

Yet another category of cleaner is the amateurs, people like students, actors, or recent emigrants from another country; these people are only doing the work until their circumstances change. They do for you what they do for themselves in their own homes. Some are remarkably capable. Most are more willing than able; to work with them effectively, you must show them exactly what you want done.

The main problem with working with independents of any kind is that few are dedicated to any one job. There are always more homes to be cleaned than there are people willing to do the work, and the pittance that we pay is not enough to command fidelity. A cleaning woman, often a working mother with young children, is dealing with all the problems of trying to fit job and home life together. When the pressures get too great, performance or attendance can become erratic or she may up and quit. Amateur cleaners, in particular, tend to be unreliable. An exam or an audition takes priority over your house any day. Should opportunity beckon, the amateur is off like a shot. When you depend on free-lancers, it is wise to stay alert to what's going on in their lives. If you suspect that they are about to move on, start thinking about what *you* are going to do next. One reason that cleaning services are proliferating is that few of us can stand the strain. The service is impersonal, it costs more, and less ground may be covered, *but* the work gets done.

A qualified cleaner generally arrives expecting to vacuum, dust, damp clean furniture, wash floors, clean visible kitchen and bathroom surfaces, and sometimes do laundry. Beyond that, it depends on the person's skills and willingness to do more. Most independents will do some, but not all, of the following: polish furniture; defrost a refrigerator; clean an oven; wax a floor; wash the insides of windows; take down and launder curtains; clean knickknacks and picture glass; and straighten out closets, bureau drawers, and medicine cabinets. Washing walls, ironing, and mending seem to be disappearing from the repertoire. On a normal day, expect an independent to do all of the major jobs along with a few of the smaller discretionary tasks or one large one (such as cleaning an oven). Expect no more of a cleaner sent by a service than what's been bargained for. If you want more, arrange for it in advance and be prepared to pay extra.

An experienced person can do the job without supervision, but it's a good idea to be there for at least a few hours on the first day to answer questions and observe techniques. Never take it for granted that a cleaning person knows more than you. Point out vulnerable surfaces, such as a leather chair or a marble tabletop, and give instructions for special care. To be on the safest side, make especially valuable things off limits and continue to maintain them yourself. Be alert to cleaning abuses. Someone who uses a dustrag to polish furniture, who spreads scouring powder on a kitchen counter, who casually sloshes water on wood is ignorant of the most elementary cleaning techniques. To avoid adverse effects, you must either try to reeducate (often easier said than done) or find someone else.

A common failing among the cleaning crowd is to use too much of any product. Watch out for laundry detergent in particular. The correct amount can be the difference between a clean wash and a dingy one, but most brands have different requirements. Get out the measuring cup and show how much to use. Don't assume that a product label will be read and its directions followed. Many cleaning people don't bother to read them; others, especially when English is not their native tongue, may not be able to. When a product is unfamiliar, explain how it should be used. Hide furniture polish and self-polishing floor wax which, no matter what the label says, are not meant to be used every time the house is cleaned.

You will always get better results if you pick up things and put them away before a cleaning person arrives. Working around clutter slows down progress. Time taken to get things out of the way is time lost. Besides, the cleaning person does not know what to do with your miscellany and simply lets your objects pile up in a corner. To get the most for your money, do your putting away before, not after.

Organize laundry yourself. Pretreat stains, separate into piles, remove anything that can be damaged by machine washing or drying. Some cleaning people are expert at doing the wash, but until you know this, don't take the chance.

Have a proper assortment of tools, cleaning agents, rags, and sponges. Some cleaning services bring their own, but most cleaners expect you to provide the right equipment. Ask a new employee if he or she has any preferences as to particular products and see to it that those products are kept in supply. Unless you are actively opposed to the use of a specific cleaning agent, it's wise to defer to the wishes of the person who is doing the work.

How much you pay depends on the going rate in your area. Cleaning services – which must cover expenses, profit, and wages – are usually more expensive than independents, although their prices for regular service are not much higher. They charge by the job and hold costs down with speedy, time-intensive cleaning methods; if a home space is not especially large, it may be finished satisfactorily in a few hours.

Independent workers also prefer to be paid by the job and tend to get everything done in four hours or less. This can mean that discretionary jobs, such as cleaning mirrors or dusting away cobwebs, are sloughed over or ignored in the rush to finish early. If this happens frequently, you miss out on the prime advantage of choosing an independent as opposed to a service – attention to detail and more jobs done. When you first hire a new cleaner, discuss your expectations and come to a mutually satisfactory agreement that includes a minimum and a maximum number of hours. On cleaning day tell your worker which jobs are to be done: post a list or call from the office if you don't meet in person. Don't overload the schedule. You know what *you* can easily accomplish in a given time. Don't expect more from your help. If you need more done, pay extra for the prolonged workday but, by the same token, if the quality slips, speak up!

People who work for you on a regular basis usually expect an extra day's pay each year in lieu of a vacation (often given around the winter holidays along with a small gift) and perhaps even a few paid sick days. The occasional raise, or bonus for jobs well done, goes a long way towards cementing employer-employee relationships.

It is hugely disappointing to come home to find a dirty house when you were expecting a clean one. If you've planned something like a dinner party for that evening, it can be a minor disaster. Impress upon your cleaning person that you need a day's notice when he or she cannot come to work. Obviously, this is not always possible and is one good reason why a home should be in reasonably good order even when a cleaning person is expected.

Other Resources
Not everyone can afford a regular cleaning

person, but this need not mean going completely without assistance. Local children can often be enlisted for specific small jobs for relatively small sums. I once paid a princely 10 cents a bag to a neighbor's son to carry out the garbage, a small but welcome assist when my apartment was a fourth floor walk-up. At another time, I hired a high school girl to come in every afternoon to pick up, make the bed, and do the dishes from the night before. It took her about an hour, and I paid the going rate for babysitting. The problem with youthful labor is that children get bored and quickly find better things to do with their free time. Working with kids is probably most productive for the occasional big job. An energetic teenager by your side during a massive cleaning effort can be a real help, especially because you are right there to supervise and boost flagging spirits.

Older people, notably women, are another resource. Many of them are getting by on woefully inadequate pensions, and extra money is badly needed. Laundry, ironing, mending, food preparation are not too taxing for most women in their 60s and any one, or all, of these services could help to make your life easier. Chances are you can work out a financial arrangement that is fair to such a woman but not prohibitive for you.

Don't overlook exchange. You and a friendly neighbor might work out a dinner arrangement in which you cook one night and he or she does the same for you the next. If you're near a college, you might offer an undergraduate home-cooked meals in return for some regular useful service. Or if you have an extra room, you might take in a boarder and accept housework as payment.

Single parents struggling under the double burden of job and home almost have to enlist friends and family when there's no money to ease the situation. Without help you risk crumbling under the load, and, if you go down, the kids go with you. Sometimes people are only waiting to be asked, afraid that if they offer to give you a hand you will consider it interference. Ask! Later on, you'll find a way to return the favors. For now, if your mother is willing to do your laundry as well as her own, let her. If your best friend doesn't mind doing a double-food shopping now and then, what's the harm? Women or men who are in the same spot can be a huge resource, providing a reciprocal back-up system that can make the hard job of raising a family on your own infinitely more easy – and a lot less lonely.

Five

Getting Food On The Table

A regular meal plan, matching good nutrition with favorite foods and available time for cooking and shopping, is the only way around the lack of time and dearth of culinary interest that often afflicts those who prepare dinner at the end of a hard day. Most busy homemakers opt for simple meals quickly made from easily accessible ingredients. Complex menus are reserved for holidays, special occasions, and those weekends or evenings when cooking feels like fun instead of drudgery. The expedient cook thinks ahead so that trips to the market are held to a minimum and learns the tricks of food storage so that supplies are there – ready and waiting – when mealtime comes.

NUTRITIONAL GUIDELINES

Proper nutrition helps to prevent stress and simple fatigue. And we know that what you do or do not eat now will influence your physical condition in the years to come. Considerations for the future are especially important for growing children and pregnant women. The supermarket magazines, *Woman's Day* and *Family Circle*, do a fine job of filtering scientific research down from the ivory tower to the popular level. Many of their articles are geared to working people and include tips for efficient menu planning as well as recipes that are nutritionally based. *Jane Brody's Nutrition Book* offers a comprehensive analysis of daily food requirements as well as advice on what should be avoided by the conscientious menu planner. There is much to know about sensible eating. Until you get the chance to do your own research, the following simple guidelines will see you through.

With a little forethought, you can easily work a good mix of essential food elements into the day's meals. But bear in mind that the concept a "balanced diet" is an artificial one, devised to provide guidance in a confused area. The body does not operate on such a rigid schedule. The off day, or even off week, does little harm. It's the day-in, year-out regime that counts. Avoid the tendency to try to cram most of the important nutrients into the evening meal. An adequately balanced diet requires an early start. Have a good breakfast, a good lunch, a normal dinner, and include honest-to-goodness nutrients in the snack plan.

There are nearly 40 elements in food that are considered essential to health. No one food provides them all. To cover all the nutritional bases, include the following in each day's menu.

4 to 6 servings from the bread-cereal group. 1 slice of bread, ½ – ¼ cup of cooked cereal, pasta, rice, or other whole grain equals a serving. Whole grains and nonrefined cereals are the richest in nutrients so include at least 1 a day. Read the label on packaged cold cereals to determine serving size; avoid cereals high in sweeteners.

4 to 6 servings from the vegetable-fruit group. 1 fruit or vegetable high in vitamin C, such as citrus fruit or juice, cantaloupe or strawberries, or broccoli, cabbage, green pepper, and 1 dark green or deep yellow vegetable should be eaten each day. Many feel it wise to include at least 1 raw vegetable as well. A portion: 1 piece of fruit such as an apple, 1 whole vegetable such as an ear of corn, a wedge of melon, ½ a grapefruit, ½ cup of juice, berries, fruit pieces, or vegetables.

2 servings from the milk group for adults, 3 for children and pregnant women, 4 for adolescents and nursing women. A cup of milk or of yogurt constitutes 1 serving. Serving sizes for other milk products are determined by the amount of calcium they contain in comparison to milk. To get an equivalent amount of calcium from cheese, it is necessary to consume 2 cups of cottage cheese, 1¼ ounces of hard cheese, such as Cheddar or Swiss, 2 ounces of cheese spread, or 1½ cups of ice cream. Calcium aside, milk and yogurt contain more nutrients than other dairy products.

2 servings from the high protein group that includes meat, poultry, fish, eggs, cheese, peanut butter, and legumes (dried beans and peas). 2 to 3 ounces of lean, cooked meat, poultry, fish, hard cheese, ½ cup of cottage cheese, 2 large eggs, 2 glasses of milk, 4 tablespoons of peanut butter, or 1 cup of legumes equals a serving. Most vegetables and all grains, nuts, seeds and some vegetables also contain protein. But, with a few exceptions, these proteins are considered incomplete and do not, in themselves, provide all of the protein elements needed by the human body. Mixing a food that contains an incomplete protein with another containing the missing components is an excellent, low-cost method of adding quality protein to the diet. 2 tablespoons of peanut

72

butter in a sandwich equals a protein serving. Rice and beans or corn and beans in succotash are high-protein vegetable dishes. Adding a small amount of animal protein to an incomplete protein is an age-old trick, which balances out the incomplete protein to provide a complete protein. Milk with cereal; spaghetti with meat sauce or grated cheese; Oriental rice-vegetable dishes that contain slivers of meat, fish, or eggs are protein-rich combinations. It's difficult to specify what constitutes a serving when foods are mixed, but what you can comfortably eat should take care of your protein needs. Unless you are operating on a hardship diet, or are a strict vegetarian, obtaining enough protein is rarely a concern; Americans tend to consume more protein than they actually need.

According to recommendations made in 1977 by the U.S. Senate Select Committee on Nutrition, at least 48 percent of the day's calories should consist of the complex carbohydrates found in cereals, grains, fruits, and vegetables, while an effort should be made to restrict saturated (mainly animal) fats, sugar, salt, and sodium. Some feel these guidelines are controversial, but most nutritionists consider them the safest rules to follow until the research into the health consequences of a diet high in saturated fat, salt, and sugar is completed.

A Few Healthful Measures: Limit eggs to 3 a week, drink skimmed milk, replace butter with margarine and cook with margarine or polyunsaturated vegetable oil. Choose uncreamed cottage cheese, low-fat yogurt, and, where possible, a lower fat cheese such as mozzarella. Substitute ice milk or sherbert for ice cream. Use cottage cheese whirled through the blender or seasoned yogurt as a substitute for mayonnaise and sour cream. Eat more poultry and fish than red meats. Remove the skin from poultry, cut the visible fat from meat before cooking, drain the fat from gravy. Use grains, pasta, and rice frequently as the major component in meals. Read labels and avoid products that put coconut oil or animal fat high on their list of ingredients. (Labels are required to list ingredients in the order of the amount contained in the product.) Avoid cold cuts that are high in fat.

To cut down on sugar and salt, curb the sweet tooth, be stingy with the salt shaker, learn to cook with flavorful spices and herbs, and read labels. Far too much of the sugar and salt we consume comes from processed foods. Don't be misled by deceptive nomenclature. Salt, sodium chloride, monosodium glutamate, hydrolyzed yeast, sea salt, and soy sauce all count as sodium; and sucrose, fructose, dextrose, turbinado, corn syrup, maple syrup, honey, and molasses are all sugars. If several of these are listed on one label, you can be sure that the salt or sugar content is high. Many packaged foods do not list ingredients. In these cases, salt or sugar may be present in significant amounts, especially when the food is canned. Canned soups, tunafish, and most vegetables, for instance, all contain high levels of added salt. When a product label claims that it is low in sugar or salt, try it, and if you like it, use it regularly. The manufacturer who yields to consumer pressure to deliver a more wholesome food deserves encouragement. Except for baking, where it is often necessary to search out health-oriented recipes, the cook can easily omit or reduce the amount of salt and sugar called for in a recipe. In fact, cutting salt and sugar in half often improves the taste of the dish, especially when ingredients are of high quality. As you wean yourself away from these additives, your taste for them will diminish to the point at which a small amount will suffice.

Once you get the knack, obtaining a balanced diet requires little effort. Consider

A FEW NUTRITIONAL POWERHOUSES

Food (a normal serving)	percentage U.S. RDA* (approximate)					
	Protein	Vitamin A	Vitamin C	Thiamin	Riboflavin	Calcuim
Cottage cheese	30	4	...	2	15	10
Broccoli	4	40	120	6	10	8
Brussels sprout; green pepper	4	10	110	4	4	2
Carrot	2	150	10	4	2	2
Greens (beet; chard; collards; kale; mustard; spinach)	2	100	50	6	10	10
Squash, winter; pumpkin	2	90	20	4	6	2
Sweet potato; yam	2	120	20	4	2	2
Apricot, canned	..	35	6	.	2	..
Cantaloupe	..	90	70	2	2	..
Grapefruit, whole; juice	..	...	70	4	2	2
Orange, whole; juice	..	4	100	6	2	4
Strawberries, raw; frozen	..	2	150	2	6	4
Tomatoes, raw; canned; juice	2	15	35	4	2	..
*Liver!***	35	500	15	10	120	..

Note: Adapted from *A Guide to Nutritive value*, a pamphlet offered by the Division of Nutritional Sciences, Cornell University, Ithaca, N.Y.

*This chart indicates a few easily obtained foods that offer an especially rich selection of essential nutrients. The U.S. RDA (recommended daily allowances) represents daily optimum allowances established by the Food and Drug

Administration. They (and the serving sizes given earlier) are based on average needs. Children require less; large men who do physical labor, more; and pregnant women have special needs.

**Because liver is also high in cholesterol, it should not be eaten more than once a week.

---

this rather nonfussy day. Breakfast consists of a bowl of cold shredded wheat, milk, and a sliced banana. Lunch is a peanut butter sandwich on two slices of whole wheat bread, with celery and carrot sticks. The mid-afternoon snack is a glass of orange juice. For dinner, a hamburger on an English muffin with a tossed salad made from lettuce, cabbage, and a generous handful of broccoli florets with a few sliced mushrooms. The late-night snack is a cup of yogurt with a peach sliced into it. That's it. The minimum requirements have been met. It could, of course, be more nutritious, but it's good enough to see you through.

SHOPPING FOR FOOD

Food shopping is a source of enjoyment for some and a hated task for others. This section is for those who want a hit-and-run technique that gets them out of the supermarket in the shortest possible time with all the essentials for the week. Those who enjoy leisurely or frequent shopping or who prefer small speciality shops are on their own.

Planning for a major shopping expedition is advised. The classic tactic calls for study of that section of the newspaper that advertises the week's specials at your favorite supermarket. A menu plan can then be drafted around featured bargains and the most plentiful produce. A quick check of the refrigerator and pantry lets you know which breakfast, lunch, and snack staples need to be replenished. The things to be purchased are then listed *according to where they can be found in the supermarket.*

Another less taxing approach forgoes a list in favor of a set food plan, the simplest of which features the same meals on a rotating basis, for example, *Week I:* Thursday, stir-fried beef and vegetables; Friday, lentil stew. *Week II:* Thursday, spaghetti with clam sauce; Friday, roast chicken. *Week III:* Thursday, stir-fried beef and vegetables; *and so on,* until it's time for a change. Anyone who pursues this plan, and shops when the store is not crowded, can shop with blinders on and get out of the supermarket in no more than ½ hour. Some shoppers may select the same standard foods every week but have several methods of preparing them so the menu can be varied.

Keep a running inventory of staples so you don't run out of essentials. The old-fashioned list pinned to the refrigerator with a magnet is probably still the easiest way to keep track of what's running low. Everyone should be responsible for keeping the list up to date; whoever used it up pencils it on the list.

Select one supermarket and shop there regularly. Memorize its floor plan. This helps you to draft a grocery list and to move throughout the store without hesitation. Be friendly with the manager so you will be recognized as a regular customer in case you want a special favor or have a complaint. Decide which checkout clerks are most efficient and frequent their registers.

Shop when inventories are high. Thursdays is usually best as the weekend specials are in stock but have yet to be picked over by other shoppers. Shop in off-hours to avoid crowded aisles and long lines. Peak traffic periods are evenings right after work, weekend afternoons, and the day before a holiday. Stores are practically empty early in the morning, although on Monday supplies may still be depleted from the weekend rush.

Shop alone or as part of a coordinated

team, especially when you're in a hurry. Companions who are there only to keep you company – and young children – slow you down and interfere with the high level of concentration that quick shopping demands.

Try to limit supermarket shopping to no more than once a week. Pick up perishables as needed, preferably at a small uncrowded store that you pass frequently on the way home. Some busy homemakers, who have perfected menu planning, manage to limit their major shopping excursions to once every 10 days or even twice a month.

Educate another member of the household to shop for food. If you're the only one who can do it, it's your job, no matter what.

GETTING THE BEST FROM THE FOOD DOLLAR

One of the biggest home responsibilities is the proper selection and care of food. Even experienced cooks often wonder if their methods of food handling are good enough to ensure food safety and preserve nutrients.

The length of time any food can be kept depends on its natural qualities, whether it has been treated to prolong its shelf life, its condition when acquired, and how it is stored. In these days of high food costs, mistakes are expensive. Buy and store foods wisely.

Meat and Poultry

A trustworthy butcher who deals in quality meat has much to offer. But this kind of shopping is obviously more expensive and less convenient than one-stop supermarket shopping, so many of us do it only on special occasions. Take advantage of those occasions and ask questions of your butcher. He or she can educate you on the finer points of meat selection.

If fresh meat of any kind is not cold to the touch, don't buy it. Avoid packages with a lot of juice collected at the bottom, evidence that the meat has been sitting around or has been frozen and defrosted. All meat should be firm to the touch with a moist, not wet, surface. Fresh *beef* is dark red in color. When tenderness is wanted, look for a fine marbling of thin white lines running through the red. This evenly distributed fat may be bad for your arteries, but it's what makes beef tender. *Lamb* can range in color from palish pink to reddish pink. Brittle fat indicates that it is past its prime or has been frozen. Look for pale whitish *pork* and reject any that is red or brown or has yellow fat. *Veal* that has a brown or gray tinge is past its prime. Look for *chicken* with moist, blemish-free skin. Avoid flesh that is brownish and dry. Skin color depends on what the bird has been fed. White or yellow are equal in taste and nutrition. Of possible interest: In a *Consumer Reports'* (May 1978) survey of chickens, brand name birds were from 9 to 14 percent more expensive than supermarket brands, but there was no discernible difference in taste or quality. *Turkey* should be plump with white – not blue or purplish – skin.

All fresh meats should be chilled as soon as possible in the coldest part of your refrigerator. As long as there is a minimum of juice, supermarket packaging is perfectly fine if the meat will be cooked that day. Otherwise, unwrap, place on a flat dish, and cover loosely so air can circulate. Tight wrapping may hasten the souring of meat or result in a bacterial growth. Chopped meat is best flattened out so that cold thoroughly permeates. Remove innards from poultry and store separately.

How long meat can be safely stored depends on its quality at the time of purchase and the chilling capacity of your refrigerator. The guidelines given in our chart (see page 93) are generally reliable, but be aware that meat and poultry are very susceptible to bacterial contamination.

Any meat can be frozen for long-term storage. Wrap tightly in freezer-weight plastic or foil; seal well. For convenience, make hamburger patties before freezing. One patty equals a hamburger, two are enough to beef up a tomato sauce, four can make a small meat loaf. To reduce fat in your diet, trim excess fat from meat and chicken and remove chicken skin before freezing. There may be some flavor loss when meats are cooked frozen, but as there is less leakage of juices, more nutrients are preserved.

Cover cooked meats well before refrigerating and plan to use them within a day or two. If you tend to hold leftovers longer than that, don't store them in the fresh foods compartment. Make individual portions, wrap in foil, label, freeze, and call them TV dinners.

Fish and Shellfish

Selecting fresh fish takes skill. The fresher the fish, the better it tastes. More often than not, though, fish offered for sale is not as fresh as it could be. Shop discriminately. Pass by any seafood that has a strong fishy or iodinelike odor. A shiny fillet that starts to fall apart when you lift it is no longer fresh. Ideally, a whole fish has bright, protruding eyes, although ice packing can cause the eye to cloud. As long as the eye is not sunk in and the scales have a good sheen and are well attached to the body, the fish should be OK.

Select firm, almost odorless, shrimp. Avoid gray or milky white scallops and choose pinkish ones that may have a yellowish tint at the edges. Reject any clams, mussels, or oysters that have cracked or open shells.

All fresh fish is highly perishable and is best used on the day of purchase or frozen. Before storing, wash with cold water. If you suspect that the fish is a bit past fresh, add a few tablespoons of lemon juice to the wash water. Wipe dry, wrap loosely, and place in the coldest part of the refrigerator. Wrap tightly for freezing. To prevent oxidation and freezer burn, glaze the fish before wrapping. To do this, dip fish or fillet in water and place it in the freezer until the water freezes. Repeat this several times to form a protective ice layer. Then, wrap and freeze normally.

Prefrozen fish, although nowhere near as tasty as fresh, is still an excellent protein source that is low in calories and polyunsaturated fats. Look for a package with no exterior staining, which indicates that contents have thawed enough to leak juice. Frozen fish sticks and breaded fillets have additional calories, salt, fat, and preservatives. They are convenient, but you may be paying for up to 50 percent breading. I personally have never seen a package of frozen shrimp worthy of the name. Buy canned shrimp and soak in cold water for 15 minutes to remove the brine.

Use cooked fish promptly or freeze.

Dairy Products and Eggs

The dairy and egg industries are so well regulated that any product you select from the supermarket shelf should be fresh enough and edible. Sell-by dates are conservative and food can almost always be used beyond the recommended day. How long beyond depends on the keeping qualities of the food and if it has been kept adequately cold. Select from the bottom of an open display case where temperatures are coldest and look for the latest sell-by date. Sour, moldy, or discolored products are spoiled, no matter what the package says.

Store milk, cream, soft cheese, and yogurt in the coldest part of the refrigerator. Do not allow them to stay at room temperature, and protect them from direct light, which destroys riboflavin. Butter and hard cheeses do best at the warmer refrigerator temperatures found on middle shelves. Keep in the original wrapping or rewrap tightly.

A smear of butter or margarine will keep the cut end of cheese from drying out. Butter, cheese, milk, and cream can be frozen. A few remaining ice crystals will make beating cream easier. The texture of milk changes when it is frozen, but this is in no way harmful and a brisk shake puts it almost right. Don't freeze a soft runny cheese before it is fully ripened.

Eggs can usually be counted on to remain good for at least 30 days after packaging, but taste diminishes with every day. Supermarket eggs are rarely the freshest. A shop that offers farm eggs is worth a side trip for those who rank flavor high. To test for freshness: Place a single egg in a large bowl of cold water. If the egg floats to the top, it's stale. It's usually best to avoid cracked eggs or any with hairline cracks, but they can, if necessary, be used in baking.

Store eggs in the egg compartment pointed end up, or in their container, on a lower refrigerator shelf. Supermarket eggs do not need to be washed before storing. Although farm eggs may appear soiled, they keep far better if they are stored unwashed.

Fruit and Vegetables
When it comes to produce, the fresher it is, the better it tastes, and the more nutrients

it contains. Shop at a market that offers crisp greens and apples; firm potatoes and onions; unshriveled lemons and garlic; white mushrooms; juicy, but not overripe, summer fruits – signs that the grocer has good purchasing judgment and storage know-how. At home, store promptly and properly to protect perishable nutrients. Fruits and vegetables contain natural enzymes that help in the ripening process, but as time passes these enzymes contribute to decay. This, along with air, heat, light, and water, destroys some vitamins and minerals. Despite the odds, even past-prime fruits and vegetables retain some food value. It's perfectly safe to remove decayed parts and eat the rest, but discard any produce that is moldy.

Store ripe fruits, unwashed, anywhere in the fridge except near the freezing element. Fruits require air, so leave them unwrapped. The skin of the fruit acts as its own nutrient-saving package. The thicker the skin, the longer the shelf life. Tough-skinned apples and pears can be kept longer than thinner skinned summer fruits such as peaches and plums. Citrus fruits can be kept for several weeks and still retain a considerable amount of vitamin C. They will stay juicier longer if kept in a cool, not cold, place; if you have no cool storage, the fridge will do. Orange or grapefruit juice kept in an opaque, covered container can be refrigerated for several days without any significant loss of vitamin C. Always sort through fruits before storing and remove any that are spoiled. For best taste, keep tomatoes at room temperature until they soften. Hard pears, nectarines, bananas, apples, and avocadoes continue to ripen as long as they remain at room temperature, but they should be refrigerated as soon as they are ready to eat. Banana skins turn black in cold, but this does not affect the fruit within. Unripe melons and fruits like peaches or plums will soften and get a bit sweeter at room temperature, but they really are best when purchased ripe and immediately refrigerated to slow enzyme action. Serve berries the day of purchase and do not cap strawberries before storing. Berries of any kind are easily frozen. Just slip the contents of the basket into a plastic bag and freeze. Store cooked, peeled, or cut fruits in sealed opaque containers; use promptly.

Don't refrigerate winter squash, yams, rutabagas, potatoes, eggplant, or yellow onions. Store unwrapped at temperatures as close to 60F. as you can find in your kitchen. Keep potatoes in a dark, dry spot where air circulates. Potatoes emit a gas that hastens the spoilage of onions, so don't put them together. Onions keep well hung in their net bags.

All other vegetables should be refrigerated. Air-tight wrappings help to keep them crisp and nutritious. The original supermarket wrap is fine as long as the seal is intact. Otherwise, closed plastic bags – the heavier the plastic, the better – are convenient, and can be used almost indefinitely. The closed vegetable bins at the bottom of the refrigerator provide the proper level of humidity and cold for most vegetables. When crisper space is at a premium, reserve it for greens, which are quickest to wilt, and cabbage, which retains nutrients for a month or longer if kept under proper conditions. All vegetables should be kept in the lower sections of the food storage compartment as they do not need coolest temperatures and are damaged by contact with the freezing unit. Leave corn in the husk and keep it uncovered outside the crisper.

It is best to wash vegetables right before serving, but it is most convenient to prewash salad greens and snacking vegetables, such as celery, before storing so they are ready for immediate use. Rinse well under cool running water and dry thoroughly for best vitamin retention. For more crispness at the cost of a small vitamin loss, allow to drain *almost* dry and wrap in a paper towel before placing into the plastic bag. To restore limp salad greens, sprinkle with cool water, wrap completely in a cloth towel, and place greens in the freezer for 10 minutes. Be sure to remove the greens before the leaves freeze. Most vegetables can be successfully frozen. Although crispness will be lost, taste and nutrients remain. Chopped onions, parsley, basil, and green peppers can be frozen as is. Most other vegetables should be blanched in boiling water before freezing.

When you are unable to shop frequently, and during winter months when most of us depend on produce that has been shipped from a distance, supplement your diet with frozen fruit juices and vegetables. Frozen produce is often processed the same day it is picked. As long as it is kept at 0°F. or below, it maintains a high vitamin and mineral content for quite some time (enzyme action is severely inhibited by low freezing temperatures). Bargains in frozen juice and produce can often be found during summer months when most people prefer fresh foods. Canned fruits and vegetables offer some food value, but not nearly as many of the necessary elements as do fresh or frozen. The high heat of the canning process diminishes the foods' heat-sensitive nutrients.

Prepare fruits and vegetables so that vitamins and minerals are preserved. Generally speaking, raw is better for you than cooked and the whole is better than pieces or juice. The largest supply of nutrients is found in or near the skin or outer leaves. Don't peel fruits and vegetables unless you must and when you do, peel thinly; use the outer leaves of greens even when they are a bit the worse for wear. Never presoak; wait to peel or dice until right before cooking.

When it comes to cooking, steaming or stir-frying is preferable to immersing in water. To stir-fry, cut vegetables in thin slices to speed up cooking and quickly coat with oil to seal nutrients in. When cooking with water, use as little as possible. Keep a cover on a steaming pot and boil water before adding fruits or vegetables. Always cook *al dente*. When you can easily detect the characteristic aroma of a fruit or vegetable, it has cooked long enough. Don't thaw frozen vegetables before cooking and don't let frozen fruits get warm and mushy before you serve them. When dinner will be delayed, put the vegetables back into the refrigerator and reheat later. Once a fruit or vegetable is cooked, it loses nutrients quickly, even in the refrigerator; freezing is preferable.

Warning note: Farmers use pesticides and weed killers, and suppliers sometimes utilize antifungicides and other preservatives to help the produce survive the trip from farm to market. Wash well any fruit or vegetable that will be eaten unpeeled. Rinse delicate greens and berries under cool running water. Scrub tough vegetables like carrots and potatoes, which can take the punishment, with a brush. Waxed green peppers and apples have a protective skin and can be gently scrubbed with diluted dishwashing liquid. Some people dip grapes, which are often treated with fungicides, repeatedly in detergent solution and rinse. Dr. Bronner's Peppermint Soap, which can be found at any health food store and many pharmacies, is soap made from natural ingredients. Many purists use it to clean all fresh produce that was not organically grown. Others peel fruits and vegetables, forgoing the vitamin bonus found in the skin, rather than add to their intake of chemicals. In truth, most of us simply rinse our produce well in plain water and hope for the best!

FOOD STORAGE CHART

Food	Refrigerate	Freeze (0°F. or below)
Fresh meats		
Beef, steaks; roasts	1–2 days	6–12 months
ground		3–4
Pork, chops		3–4
roasts		4-8
fresh sausage		1–2
Veal/Lamb, chops; steaks		6–9
roasts		
Stew Meat, any kind		3–4
Liver		3–4
Poultry		
Chickens, whole		12 months
parts		9
Turkey, whole		12
parts		6
Giblets		3
Fish	1–2 days	6–9 months
Shrimp		2
Shellfish		3–6
Cured Meats		
Ham, whole	1 week	1–2 months
half	3–5 days	1–2
canned	1 year	don't
Bacon	1 week	2–4
Corned Beef	7 days	2 weeks
Sandwich Meat, sealed, opened	7 days	don't
Sausage, smoked	3–5 days	don't
Some Cooked Foods		
Chicken, Turkey		
in broth or gravy	1–2 days	6 months
plain	1–2 days	1

93

Food	Refrigerate	Freeze (0°F. or below)
Beef, Lamb, Pork	3–4 days	2–3
Meat Loaf	2–3 days	3
Spaghetti Sauce	3–4 days	6–8
Fish	2–3 days	1
Pot Pies	1–2 days	2–3
Chicken, Egg, Tuna salad	1–2 days	don't

This (somewhat modified) chart is used with the permission of *Family Circle Magazine*.

Frozen Foods

The quality of store-bought frozen foods depends mainly on the care it is given by the people who handle it. Avoid anything that looks as though it might have thawed and been refrozen; select packages that are solidly frozen; get the food into your own freezer as soon as you can. Complain to the store manager if you find ice crystals inside the package or if the food tastes stale when you prepare it. The mishandling may have occurred before it reached the store, but if it happens often, then buy your frozen foods elsewhere.

The freezer is a great time saver. Tips for using it to advantage are scattered throughout the sections on food, and precautionary measures are discussed under food safety.

Canned, Packaged, and Bottled Goods

Unopened cans and packages can remain safe for a long time, but gradually lose flavor and nutrients. There's no absolute deadline for these items, but 12 to 18 months is probably the limit. They will keep better and longer in temperatures of 50–60° F. Accidental freezing may change the texture, but the food remains safe to eat. Provide dry storage. Dampness causes a can to rust and a package to self-destruct. A rusted or dented can remains safe so long as it does not leak. Dispose of any can that leaks or bulges (do not taste the contents).

Once a package is opened, protect the food from air and moisture, which can hasten spoilage, by transferring it to a covered canister or glass jar. A tight-fitting top will help to discourage insects. Don't buy large economy sizes unless you know they will be used quickly. Coffee, flour, cookies and crackers, whole grain cereals (such as oatmeal), and brown sugar will last longer in the freezer.

Flour, whole grains, and cereals are best used within a month as these products turn rancid at room temperature once the original seal is broken. Rancid food won't make you sick, but they are not as good for you as they should be.

Herbs lose flavor quickly when exposed to air, light, or heat. These food enhancers are becoming expensive enough that tossing them out when they are stale hurts the pocketbook. Share with a friend to split the cost and don't keep them near the stove.

Never store an open food package under the sink. It's usually the first place to be visited by rodents and insects, and there's always the possibility of water leakage.

Almost all canned, jarred, and bottled foods should be considered perishable once the seal is broken. Refrigerate them. Some canned products, such as ham or soft cheese, must be refrigerated even when they are unopened. When a product is new to you, check the label.

Cooking and salad oils and oily foods like peanut butter should be refrigerated to forestall rancidity. Oils turn cloudy and thicken in the refrigerator, but this is a temporary effect. A few minutes at room temperature restores pouring or spreading consistency. An opened bottle of mayonnaise *must* be refrigerated promptly.

In humid weather, keep bread in the refrigerator. Otherwise, store at room temperature. Bread freezes well for longer keeping.

Health note: Sometimes the solder used to seal cans contains lead, and significant amounts of that lead can find their way into canned food. As long as the can remains sealed, there is little cause for concern. However, once a can is opened it's another matter, especially when the food contains a significant amount of acid. The references that suggest it is OK to store foods in an open can are *out of date.*

A FAST FOOD PLAN

There are fast and slow ways to do just about anything. When it comes to cooking, the slow ways are often most satisfying but not when you have other things to do or are bone weary. Here are a few speedy routines and shortcuts to fall back on when time is tight or energy short:

Establish a set weekday breakfast menu. Cold cereal, milk, and fruit are the easiest. Read labels to determine which cereals are the most nutritious and keep an assortment of favorites on hand. Hot cereal can be made in minutes. Another simple start-the-day repast is sliced cheese on bread. For variety, it takes only a few minutes to melt the cheese under the broiler, and in a pinch it can be eaten on the way out the door. So can bread and peanut butter.

If you "brown bag it," try to make lunch the night before and store it in the refrigerator. Establish a few favorite lunches and vary them just enough to keep them from becoming boring. Peanut butter and cottage cheese are good high-protein spreads for bread; banana or apple slices or a sprinkling of raisins add interest. Sliced turkey, meat loaf, or chicken are better for you than commercial cold cuts. Include a piece of fruit and a raw finger vegetable such as cherry tomatoes or green pepper strips to make sure you get your daily allotment of vitamins and minerals. Pack perishables with a prechilled jel-pack to keep them safe. A cup of yogurt is the equivalent of a glass of milk. It's not lunch.

Develop a repertoire of fast cooking or low attention dinners and include some that are simple enough so that anyone in the house can prepare them. Keep the ingredients on hand. The country and peasant style dishes created by farm wives, who had other things to do besides stand by the stove, are often easy on the cook. Marian Burros is a nutritionally aware food writer who combines interest in gourmet foods with expediency.

Her *Keep It Simple* is a cookbook for meals that can be prepared in a half hour.

If you do any job often, then analyze it and figure out how to do it quickly. Learn how to wield a chopping knife and how to dice an onion. Use your hand as a measuring tool. Measure a tablespoon of oregano into your palm and study it. Repeat until you know what a tablespoon's worth of something looks like. Use the same pots for repeat jobs like cooking rice or vegetables and learn to judge the right amount of water visually.

Cook with cleanup in mind. Collect recipes that make little mess. Learn how your stove and cookware work together and control cooking temperatures so you won't burn food onto the pot or boil it over onto the stove. Clean as you go and don't let hard-to-clean substances, like batter or raw egg, dry in the pot or on the counter top. Fill a dishpan with warm soapy water and drop used utensils in to soak as you finish with them. Keep a small portable garbage container, such as an empty milk container or a plastic scrap bag, near you as you work.

Establish an energy-sparing serving routine. Many cooks prefer to prepare the food and have self-service in the kitchen. Sandwiches are only a convenience if you don't have to prepare them for a crowd. Let the crowd make their own; just put the fixings out for them. At the end of the meal, let each diner be responsible for personal cleaning up.

Use your freezer to good advantage. Prepare big batches of spaghetti sauce, cook the whole head of broccoli or the entire box of rice. Ladle meal-sized amounts into heavy plastic bags, seal tightly, and freeze. Make double or more recipes to freeze for later. If there's only one of you, or your household tends to eat in shifts, freeze individual portions. Plastic sandwich bags are a convenient small container, but they are not thick enough to prevent freezer burn. For more protection, place several portions into a larger plastic bag.

Use foil-wrapping so you can slip frozen food into the oven and reheat it without messing up a pot. To freeze foods with a high liquid content, use any suitably sized container as a mold. Line it with freezer-weight foil, with enough overlap to cover the food, pour the food in, seal the foil, and freeze. When it's solid, remove the foil packet from the container and stack it in the freezer. Label packages so you'll know what's hidden inside. Reheat in a 350–375° oven. Foil sometimes leaks, so place the foil-wrapped food into an ovenproof receptacle first.

Consider the refrigerator's freezer a labor-saving device. Most cooked foods can be frozen successfully, so there's practically no end to what the resourceful cook can manage.

Pasta has become the new convenience food now that everyone realizes that it's not as fattening as once thought and that it's good for you besides. Save time by lessening the amount of water you use. A 2½ or 3 quart saucepan, almost filled with water, is large enough to cook ½ pound of pasta. If you break spaghetti in half and pour a little oil on top of the water before adding the pasta, few if any strands will stick together.

Quickie dressings for pasta:
Olive oil or butter and grated cheese.

White clam sauce prepared by lightly browning two large diced cloves of garlic in oil, to which a can of clams with broth are added along with a handful of chopped raw parsley; simmer 10 minutes. For variety, sauté summer squash and onions before adding the clams.

Grated Swiss or Muenster cheese and a handful of caraway seeds mixed with hot pasta.

Yogurt and raw chopped scallions, minced parsley, or basil, or a combination of the herbs mixed with hot pasta.

Vegetables such as zucchini or broccoli

florets can be cooked in tomato sauce or stir-fried with garlic in oil and tossed with grated cheese into hot pasta.

Cheese is a standby that can usually be found in the refrigerator. Baked potatoes heaped with cottage cheese and lots of pepper are an easy main dish. Cottage or grated cheese mixed with any hot vegetable will boost a meal's protein content as will a handful of sesame seeds. For an oven cheese melt, slice cheese into a shallow ovenproof dish that can go right to the table and slip it into a slow (325°) oven. A mix of cheese such as Cheddar or colby or Muenster and Swiss works well. Bake just until the cheese melts; don't overcook. Pour off the melted butterfat and place the pot in the center of the table along with crisp bread. Let everyone dip.

Some cooks find it difficult to fit fruits and vegetables into the menu. *A few suggestions:*

Any vegetable can be cooked in foil along with whatever else might be baking in the oven. Dot the vegetable with butter (no more than a teaspoon needed), sprinkle with a teaspoon of water, season, and seal foil tightly. Bake 20 to 45 minutes depending on the thickness of the vegetable and the heat of the oven. To speed things up, slice vegetables thin.

To bake sweet and white potatoes, beets

or onions, string them onto a shish kebab skewer. This cuts cooking time by about $\frac{1}{3}$.

Any vegetable can be added to steaming rice during the last 15–20 minutes of cooking time. Frozen peas can be stirred in after the rice is done; the heat of the rice is enough to warm them through.

Premix your salad dressings. A mix of $\frac{1}{3}$ of a cup of mayonnaise, $\frac{2}{3}$ of a cup of yogurt, and a teaspoon of dill or mustard, or both, is tasty and will keep several days in the refrigerator.

Sliced fruits such as pears, apples, oranges, or grapefruit, add variety to green salads. So do hulled pumpkin seeds.

Don't overlook the mealtime beverage as a way of adding vitamins and minerals to the diet. Diluted frozen fruit juice is refreshing, as is a generous squeeze of lime or lemon in seltzer or plain water.

It isn't how long a meal takes to cook that counts but the time you spend preparing it. Slow cookers that fix in minutes and need little or no attention until they're done are often quite delicious. Here are a few:

Lentil stew: 1 cup of lentils, 2 onions, 4 carrots. Cut into large pieces. Add a stalk or 2 of diced celery and any vegetables you have in the fridge such as cabbage, along with a can of tomato pieces, and/or a can of chicken broth and 3 or 4 cups of water. Sprinkle in a tablespoon of dill and cook until lentils are soft and the mixture tastes like stew (about 1½ hours). Serve with a dollop of sour cream. Serves 4. Freezes well.

Oven chowder: Slice 2 onions and 3 potatoes and put them in the bottom of a baking dish. Place fish (frozen or thawed) on top, cover with milk and stir in 2 tablespoons of grated Parmesan cheese. Bake uncovered in a 325° oven until potatoes are soft. Right before serving, stir a generous handful of frozen peas into the sauce. Serves 3.

Oriental-style chicken: Place a quartered chicken (or an equivalent amount of any chicken parts) into a large casserole. Add a can of sliced water chestnuts, 2 quartered onions, 3 cut-up carrots, and 2 green peppers cut into large slices. Sliced sweet potatoes, broccoli florets, cabbage leaves, or whole mushrooms can also be used. Pour a mix of ½ small can of frozen orange juice, 3 tablespoons of tamari soy sauce (a bit lower in sodium than other soy sauces), ½ teaspoon of garlic powder, and 1 cup of water over the chicken and vegetables. Cover and bake in a 325° oven until the chicken is tender (about 1½ hours; allow and extra ½ hour if chicken is frozen). Serves 3–4.

Tzimmes: This is a company meal that can be extended to feed a number of guests simply by boiling more potatoes and slivering the meat instead of slicing it. Early in the day cut 2 bags of carrots into thin vertical slices, or leave carrots whole if time is short. Put into a large heavy pot and add a 4-pound brisket of beef, 12 dried prunes, 1 sliced onion, and 5 whole black peppercorns. Barely cover with water. Bring to a rolling boil, then reduce to a simmer. Cook covered over a low flame for about 4 hours or until the meat is fork tender and easily shredded. Serve with boiled potatoes, 2 to 3 for each person eating. Feeds 6 people generously and 10 to 12 people adequately. For larger numbers, be sure to have plenty of bread and make a substantial salad. Can be prepared the day before and reheated.

A few simple, almost healthful, desserts:
Slice bananas and apples together in a casserole, dot with butter or margarine, and sprinkle lightly with brown sugar. Cover and bake in a 350° oven for 30 minutes.

One frozen pie crust, filled with quartered, *unpeeled* apples or pears, or a combination of the two, dotted with butter or margarine, dusted with cinnamon, sprinkled lightly with brown sugar and a teaspoon of milk, is a pretty good imitation of a pie. Place a piece of foil slightly larger than the pie pan on the oven rack under the pie to catch juice run-off. Cover fruit lightly with foil and bake in a 450° oven for about 20 minutes.

Food for thought: Most of the above recipes have been adapted from standard cookbook recipes because ingredients were missing from my pantry or there was not enough time to do it "right." None of them is in any way as precise as it may appear in print, so the recipes can be varied easily depending upon what's on hand or how tired the cook is. When using a recipe, it's rarely necessary to follow exact directions. A little more or a little less tomato sauce or chopped onion really doesn't matter. One meat, seasoning, or vegetable can often be substituted for another as long as tastes are complementary. Be precise, however, when measuring salt, sugar, and high-calorie fats and oils and follow directions when baking failure-prone cakes, breads, and souffles. Otherwise, practice good judgment and don't be afraid to experiment. The limits of adaptive cooking soon become apparent. In the course of any cooking lifetime, far more meals are ruined by forgetting to take the pot off the stove than by expedient innovations.

Most foods that reach our kitchens are safe to eat, and the majority of cooks operate with adequate controls to prevent severe incidents of food poisoning. When it does ocur, food poisoning is usually no more serious than a short bout with a virus (for which it is often mistaken). Bacterial food poisoning, however, can be fatal, especially to the elderly, and is a cause for concern. There is no hard-and-fast reassuring rule to determine whether "it" is safe to eat, and there is rarely any discernible evidence that dangerous microbes or their toxins are present. But there are guidelines that can help you make an intelligent decision.

Bacteria thrive in most foods that are high in protein and low in acid. Meats, fish, poultry, eggs, and milk – and foods made from them – are most prone to contamination. The safest foods include dry products, such as flour, rice, uncooked legumes, and those including an abundant acid substance like vinegar, tomato, or lemon. Fruits and vegetables present no health risk unless they have been improperly canned or are moldy. Foods permeated with salt and sugar or modern preservatives are less vulnerable to bacterial action, but this varies from product to product. Consult package labels for storage guidelines.

Bacteria that doesn't get into food in the first place can't cause trouble. Patronize clean shops and keep kitchen surfaces and implements clean. Wash your hands with soap before cooking and after handling raw meat or poultry. Porous wooden cutting boards and butcher block counters provide optimum conditions for bacterial growth. When such a surface has been saturated with a protein-rich food – especially the juice of raw or rare meat, fish, or poultry – disinfect it with full-strength chlorine bleach or scour with hot water and table salt.

The best safeguard against food poisoning is time and temperature control. Keep hot foods *hot* and cold foods *cold;* refrigerate perishables promptly. Bacteria multiply rapidly in temperatures that have reached 45–140° F. Growth is especially rapid at 60–120° F., and susceptible foods that have remained at these temperatures for two hours should be discarded. These temperatures are cumulative and include time spent getting groceries from the store to the refrigerator, from refrigerator to the stove, and from stove to dinner plate. Although cooking temperatures (165° and over) quickly kill most bacteria, they cannot be counted on as a safeguard if foods have remained too long in the danger zone, as toxins produced by some microbes are not destroyed by heat. Be sure, as well, that your refrigerator is cold enough to do its job. Ideally, this is 35–38° F. on the coldest shelf, although 40° F. is acceptable. Just a few degrees higher, and a refrigerator becomes a breeding ground for bacteria.

Refrigeration slows bacterial development but does not stop it; use perishables promptly. Make sure that large quantities of warm food chill through quickly, as there is some risk that internal temperatures will remain in the danger zone long enough for bacteria to reach toxic levels. Divide food into smaller portions, store in a flat container, or precool by setting the contained food into a sink of ice water, occasionally stirring the food with a clean spoon.

Freezing stops the growth of microbes, so frozen foods remain as safe to eat as they were at the time they were frozen. But because freezing temperatures cannot be counted on to kill bacteria, you should assume that any dangerous bacteria present before freezing are still there, ready to resume activity once food is thawed. It is safest to defrost frozen items inside the refrigerator. When time is too short for this, seal the food in a plastic bag and place in cold water, changing the water frequently to keep it cold.

Foods that have thawed can usually be safely refrozen if they still retain ice crystals or have remained at temperatures no higher than 40° F. for no longer than 48 hours, but caution is indicated. The deciding factor is how well the food was handled before freezing and how quickly it froze through. Commercially frozen foods are generally safer than those frozen at home. Refrigerator freezing units are less reliable than free-standing models. Always cook any high-protein food that has been thawed and refrozen *thoroughly!* Because eating quality is usually diminished, you may prefer to cook thawed food before refreezing. Don't refreeze ice cream or fish, and discard anything that smells or looks "off." Should the freezer stop working, keep its door closed. Generally, a full freezer will hold foods frozen for two days; one that is half full, for a day.

Cook foods that are susceptible to bacterial activity thoroughly. When roasting large cuts of meat, a meat thermometer inserted into the thickest part of the meat – avoiding any bone – is the surest way of determining that the meat is done (see temperature chart). For thinner cuts, cook until the meat is warmed

COOK TO TEMPERATURE SHOWN
(Thermometer Inserted into Meat)

	Fahrenheit
Fresh Beef	
Rare	140
Medium	160
Well Done	170
Fresh Veal	170
Fresh Lamb	
Medium	170
Well Done	180
Fresh Pork	170
Cured Pork	
Ham, Raw	
(Cook before eating)	160
Ham, Fully cooked	
(Heat before serving)	140
Shoulder	
(Cook before eating)	170
Poultry	
Turkey	180–185
Boneless	
Turkey Roasts	170–175
Stuffing	
(Inside or	
outside the bird)	165

This chart gives the U.S. Department of Agriculture's suggested guidelines for roasted meat. To be on the safe side, follow them. They guarantee that illness-causing bacteria and parasites are destroyed. Many cooks feel that meats cooked to these temperatures are too well done, but lower temperatures are not recommended by health authorities.

through. The cautious cook will forgo blood-rare meat and settle for pink. Pork and poultry should always be cooked until no trace of pink remains, although meat closest to the bone sometimes retains a reddish cast no matter how long it's cooked. This is not of concern. Always heat ground meat until it is at least brownish pink at the center. Because it is handled so often in preparation and because the grinding process distributes bacteria completely through the meat, ground meat is one of the riskier of the high-protein foods. When preparing patties that are still frozen, cook them to well done to compensate for the lowered internal temperatures. Whenever you cook a high protein dish in a frozen state, give it a little extra cooking time to give heat a chance to permeate.

Because stuffed poultry is so often implicated in incidents of food poisoning, prepare it with care. Wash the cavity of the bird and dry with paper towels before refrigerating. Remove innards and store separately. Stuff poultry just before roasting and pack stuffing loosely. Don't let a stuffed bird remain at room temperature, before or after it is cooked; remove stuffing before refrigerating. Authorities suggest that you cook dressing in a separate pan, especially when the bird weighs more than 15 pounds.

Botulin – the most dangerous of the toxins – is, with a few rare exceptions, only a threat when foods have been improperly canned. Follow all recommended procedures when canning food yourself. Do not use an old cookbook; its guidelines are almost certainly out of date. The U.S. Department of Agriculture recommends that home-canned vegetables be boiled for 10 minutes before eating, and spinach, corn, meat, or poultry for at least 20 minutes. When it comes to store-bought goods, your best protections are the extremely strict industry regulations imposed by government agencies and the devastating effects of fatal carelessness on a company's finances. While botulin does not usually advertise its presence, to be on the safe side select cans that are in good condition, avoiding any that bulge or leak. A dented can is safe to use as long as it is intact at seams and rim. Dispose of foods that smell bad, are discolored, foam or spurt from the can when you open it. *Do not under any circumstances taste a suspect food.* One-millionth of a gram of botulin can kill. There is a rare form of botulism caused by contaminated honey that has no effects on children or adults but may be harmful to infants. Do not use honey to prepare baby formula.

The effects of molds and their chemical by-products on the human organism are under suspicion. Dispose of any moldy food, unless it is an old friend like bleu cheese. Do not cut away the obvious mold and serve the rest. The whole food may be contaminated.

To sum up: Buy food from conscientious merchants; keep food clean; keep it cold or hot enough; when in doubt, throw it away, *untasted.*

KITCHEN PESTS

Insects and rodents are unwelcome, hungry guests that can ruin good food and spread disease. To discourage their visits, wash dishes promptly; keep food covered; keep the lid on the garbage pail; clear any remaining pet food after your pet has eaten its fill. Be alert should you see *a* mouse or *a* roach. These creatures breed so quickly that they can get out of hand almost before you realize you have a problem.

Roaches can sometimes be controlled with a mixture of $\frac{2}{3}$ boric acid and $\frac{1}{3}$ sugar. Spread it under the sink, a favorite spot for roaches, and wherever you've seen the insects. A trace of boric acid will not do you any harm, but it is a poisonous substance. Do not use it where a child might be tempted to try a sample. Spraying is often more effective than boric acid, but all sprays are very toxic! Protect food and dishes and clean food preparation surfaces after each use. For a major infestation, it is necessary to empty the kitchen shelves and spray thoroughly. Be prepared to follow up with another spray in a few weeks. Roaches are marvels of adaptive survival. When a pregnant female is killed – and most females seem to be pregnant most of the time – she lays eggs prematurely, leaving a new batch of tiny descendants to take up where she left off. When your efforts no longer seem to be effective, switch to another product. Your resident bugs have become immune to the spray.

The old-fashioned mousetrap is still the best approach to mouse control if the rodent is not too smart to go for the bait. Spread peanut butter or sticky cheese over the trigger and place the trap at a right angle to the wall near where you suspect the mouse is denning. A single mouse is a charming animal that would make a perfect wild pet *if* it were the only one. Chances are if you've seen one, you already have at least a pair and soon you will be inundated. Prepare yourself to be cruel or use a Have-a-Heart trap to catch the animals live and dispose of them well away from your house; mice have a strong homing instinct. Prepackaged poison mousetraps are another alternative if spring traps don't do the job. Place them where children or pets can't get at them. If you are unable to control mice or roaches, call a pro. Find one who guarantees results and get a personal referral from a satisfied customer. Don't try to handle rats yourself. These are not big mice but very shrewd, tough creatures that are potentially dangerous. Call an exterminator or query the local board of health for advice.

Flies are best controlled by putting screens at the windows. If you cannot manage this and have a summer problem, use flypaper in the kitchen and keep a fly swatter handy. Aerosol poisons sprayed into the air are not recommended, and the foil-wrapped hanging devices should never be used anywhere near where food is eaten or prepared.

Six

Putting The Kitchen
To Work For You

An active cook can easily walk a city block in the course of preparing one normal meal in a normal-sized kitchen; a complex dinner made in a large kitchen can add up to a quarter of a mile! Much of this back-and-forth – plus a lot of bending, stretching, and searching for implements – just isn't necessary. Organization is the essential labor-saving strategy. With it, even a spatially inadequate kitchen can become a happier work place.

An efficient kitchen has defined job centers where tasks are coordinated to align with the physical layout of the space. These centers should be as near as possible to the major fixture – stove, sink, refrigerator – that is used most often to get the job done. Ideally a center contains only those things needed for the activity, placed conveniently within reach of the area. Nonessentials are kept well away from the field of action. In a centered kitchen, all repetitive operations, from coffee

117

brewing to salad making, can be carried out in energy-sparing fashion. Think of it as a factory in which you are the only moving part of the assembly line. Work through your procedures to reduce motion (and to confine mess to selected areas).

In most kitchens, primary centers are created for food preparation and cooking. Depending on the needs of the household, secondary centers are also established for such continuing activities as food storage or salad preparation.

A *food preparation center* should be near the stove so the cook can tend to food on the stove while assembling ingredients and mixing other parts of the meal. We'll assume you have counter space near the stove where the work can be done, along with accessible storage space and electric outlets. Store dried and canned foods here, along with small appliances and necessary implements such as mixing bowls, casseroles, measures, and so forth. This area can easily become too crowded, and it's best to limit it to activities relating to the stove or main-meal preparation. To free space, a toaster and juicer, along with dry cereal and bread, might be placed near the refrigerator, for instance.

A well-organized *cooking center* keeps

necessary cooking accessories and utensils handy to the stove. A cooking center should always include a heat resistant pot rest; a selection of thick pot holders; and a product for putting out a fire, either a small kitchen extinguisher or an easy-to-reach large container of a flame-smothering substance such as salt or baking soda.

A *vegetable preparation/salad center* is most conveniently placed near the source of water. Chopping block and knife, paring knife, salad bowl, vegetable steamer and peeler, scrub brush, as well as vinegar and salad seasonings, belong next to the sink. This is also a good spot for the food processor or blender, but make sure that the cords do not come into contact with water and work the equipment with dry hands.

Food storage is another repeat activity that works well near the sink where many cooks rinse vegetables before refrigerating them and leftovers are carried from the table to the dishwashing area. An assortment of plastic wrap and bags, foil and storage bowls, and a small work space are all that's needed to center this activity.

Tips to help make a center work:
° If something is used in only one place, keep it there. A colander, for instance, is

119

generally related to water. Store it by the sink.

° Keep movable objects close to where they are used first in food preparation. Some pots and pans should find a home by the stove, but the coffee pot and vegetable steamer are needed first at the sink. Casseroles and baking tins belong naturally near the work counter where ingredients are assembled.

° When placement is optional, store objects where they are used most frequently. Decide whether the mixing bowl that is also a handy serving utensil is wanted most often for food preparation or for serving; store accordingly. When something always seems to be needed in two places, get a duplicate of that item.

° Things that are used together should go together. When the coffee pot is stored *with* the coffee and its measurer, coffee making becomes a simple, one-step operation. If the convenient space for the coffee pot and ingredients is the cabinet above the sink (where you already store your everyday china), move a few plates to one side to make room.

° Frequently used utensils should be accessible. If you need the big bowl every day, don't stack it with a number of smaller bowls, which must be removed before you can get at the big bowl. Save convenient hanging space for tools that are in constant demand. If you're short of hanging space, consider the new plastic-covered wire grids that offer flexible storage advantages and are easily washed, unlike pegboard, which is a grease trap.

° Unless you have an extremely spacious kitchen, don't block your work counters with articles that are not used daily, such as a radio or toaster. *Exception:* If you are trying to work a new appliance into your routines, the more conveniently it is placed, the more likely you are to put it to use.

° It is sometimes difficult to establish a new order in a long-established kitchen. One way of getting a fresh perspective is to move *everything* (except perishable food) out of the kitchen and put it somewhere else, such as the living room floor. Be prepared to leave it there for at least a week while you go about your normal kitchen routines, carrying items back into the kitchen only as they are needed. In the process, you will notice where things are generally used, and appropriate placement will come clear. At the end of the week, consider the items that have not yet been returned to the kitchen and ask yourself, "Do I really want this?" If the answer is yes, assign the article to out-of-the-way storage, because it is not part of your normal routine. If the answer is no, get rid of it. Once you've eliminated nonessentials, it is much easier to regroup the tools you need.

IMPROVING THE SPACE

Given the Solomon's choice between a too large or too small kitchen, most experienced cooks opt for a compact model that allows the chef to function within easy reach of stove, sink, and refrigerator. Because small kitchens inevitably mean skimpy work surfaces and inadequate storage, busy cooks modify them to include fold-up or portable counters and extra shelves and hanging devices (bulky extra equipment, like the oversized company coffee pot, may be kept in another part of the house). To gain extra work space, wooden boards can be cut to fit the top of the stove or sink and stored away when not in use. A narrow board placed across the sink allows water to be run at the same time food is prepared. Hints to increase space and efficiency are abundant in newspaper home sections and house-oriented magazines.

Large kitchens present a problem that is

often not recognized. Unless these kitchens are well organized, they are tiring places in which to work! When there is too much room, the cook is likely to be in constant motion, hard put to do two jobs at once. An easy solution is a mobile cart with a work-proof surface such as butcher block. This maneuverable device can serve as a portable work center, allowing the cook to move jobs closer together. A centrally located worktable is another step saver. Take advantage of the large space to have at least one center where you can sit and work comfortably.

Work and storage space is dictated by the placement of the stove, sink, and refrigerator. For most of us, the sink is a permanent fixture, but it is often possible to move the stove or refrigerator. When making adjustments, consider the sink the most used area in the kitchen. Anything you can do to improve its utility will serve you well. Counter space on either side aids in dishwashing routines and helps to keep food separate from dirty dishes. Counters can be quite compact and still helpful.

When adjusting a work area near the stove, try to give yourself enough room; a spacious counter top makes work much easier, cuts down on confusion and allows a cook to utilize a number of small appliances. Ensure that wiring is adequate and that there are enough outlets. A smaller counter covered with a heat resistant material could become a convenient pot rest and a holding area for cooked foods.

If one of your major appliances must have an inconvenient location, make it the refrigerator. This is used much less often than either the stove or the sink and an efficient cook soon learns to limit steps by removing everything that's needed from the refrigerator at one time.

A good source of ideas for kitchen modification is *The Kitchen Book* by Terence Conran.

THE BIG THREE: REFRIGERATOR/FREEZER, STOVE, KITCHEN SINK

The modern refrigerator, stove, and sink (along with its ever-ready supply of hot running water) are among the wonders of modern times. Don't miss out on any of your blessings. Learn to use your big kitchen aids to full, efficient advantage and make time to read the pamphlets on their care and use supplied by the manufacturers.

Refrigerator/Freezer
The key to refrigerator efficiency is

controlled low temperature. Temperatures between freezing and 40° F. inhibit the bacterial growth and enzyme action that cause vulnerable foods to decay. To check whether your refrigerator is doing its job, taste the milk. If it's really cold, you've got nothing to worry about; just use perishables within a reasonable period of time. If milk is only coolish to warm and if matters don't improve when you adjust the dial downwards or defrost, call the repairman. A too-warm refrigerator is a breeding ground for the bacteria that cause food poisoning. For a most accurate reading, place a refrigerator thermometer on the shelf closest to the freezing unit and take an overnight reading.

Freezing temporarily stops bacterial growth and severely inhibits enzyme action. This allows most foods to be held safely almost indefinitely so long as freezing temperatures are maintained. The optimum temperature for long-term storage is 0° F. or below, but some refrigerator freezers, especially those found in one-door units, can't maintain temperatures this low. Higher temperatures present no health risk so long as foods actually remain frozen, but quality, which diminished eventually even under the best freezing conditions, diminishes more rapidly at higher freezing temperatures. If ice cream turns soft overnight, don't expect to hold other foods for any length of time. If ice cream – one of the most difficult foods to freeze – stays hard, other foods will present no problem. Trial and error is the best way to determine the keeping abilities of your refrigerator's freezer, but most of today's units can be counted on to keep food edible from one shopping trip to the next.

To help your unit do its best work:

° Don't open doors any more often than necessary and don't let them stand open, especially on hot, humid days. Make it a habit to limit your trips to the refrigerator. When preparing a meal, remove all refrigerated items at one time, but don't let perishable items stay out long enough to get warm.

° Cover foods so that moisture does not evaporate from them into the refrigerator's interior.

° Let cold air circulate freely. Don't overcrowd shelves or stack foods. Leave some space between containers and between refrigerator walls and containers.

° Try not to stand a refrigerator next to the stove or other heat source unless that heat source has such effective insulation that it will block heat transference, as in the case of a modern wall oven.

° When frost accumulations are $\frac{1}{4}''$ – $\frac{1}{2}''$ thick, defrost. A heavier buildup increases your electric bill and decreases cooling effectiveness. Two-door units rarely have to be defrosted more than 3 or 4 times a year. Single-door models may need defrosting as often as once a month. Frost-free refrigerators never need to be defrosted, but they are quite costly to run.

Establish a refrigerator routine. Keep staples highly visible so you can tell at a glance when they need to be replaced. Keep extremely perishable items, and those whose shelf-life is about to run out, right up front so you will remember to use them. If you store frozen foods for any length of time, mark them with dates so they can be used while they are still at their best. Keep small jars and bottles on door racks, which are designed to keep them erect and visible. Wrap aromatic foods well. Group items that are used together or serve similar purposes, such as cheeses, condiments, and beverages.

The degree of cold varies throughout the refrigerator. The coldest temperatures are found nearest the freezer, the warmest toward the bottom of the food storage compartment. The back and bottom of the freezing compartment is usually colder than the front and top. Assign coldest refrigerator space to most perishable foods and give coldest freezer space to those you plan to keep longest.

The holding devices provided with the refrigerator (egg and butter compartments, vegetable crispers, and the like) provide optimum levels of cold and humidity for the foods they are designed to hold. Plastic wrap and bags, or aluminum foil give adequate protection to most frozen and refrigerated foods, although for long-term freezer storage a double wrap with foil or two plastic bags will help to prevent freezer burn.

Make a point of mopping up spills and drip marks and covering foods well to keep odors from escaping, so you won't have to do a big clean more than once a year. *Exceptions:* The drain under the crisping bins and the catch pan beneath the refrigerator. Wash the pan once a month after pouring a little chlorine bleach down the drain.

Use any mild cleaning solution to clean the outside of your refrigerator. Vacuum refrigerator coils frequently. If you let the coils go too long, you may have to hire a professional repairman to do the job or live with a refrigerator that has diminished cooling ability. Sometimes coils are hidden beneath the fridge. These can be partially vacuumed from the front when the decorative floor grid is removed. At least once a year, more often if dust is a problem in your area, pull the box away from the wall and vacuum from the rear.

To clean the inside of a refrigerator, turn controls to off. Take out the removable parts and soak these in lukewarm soapy water. Wash and deodorize the interior with a solution of one tablespoon baking soda in a quart of warm water. Stuck-on spots will come up easier if you soften with a wet paper towel and then clean with a plastic scrubber. Rinse everything and wipe dry. Don't use extremely hot water on refrigerator plastic, or it will crack.

Defrosting is usually listed as a most hated household task, but it is a rather simple job, especially if you don't put it off too long. Although manufacturers recommend that the job should be done when frost accumulation is between $\frac{1}{4}''$ and $\frac{1}{2}''$ thick, firsthand experience indicates that nothing much happens if you delay a bit; but there is no denying that prompt attention means far less work.

The following general guidelines apply for a standard two-door refrigerator/freezer with the freezer on top. If your model is different, check the manufacturer's manual for appropriate instructions.

To defrost

Turn controls to off.

Unload frozen foods into a picnic cooler and empty the contents of the ice cube trays on top. A double-thick brown paper bag will also serve as an insulating container. Either will keep foods cold enough for a few hours. *Exception:* Ice cream melts. (Keep the door to the refrigerator section closed and fresh food will stay cool enough.)

Spread newspapers on the floor in front of the refrigerator and along the path to the sink. Line the bottom of the freezer with several thicknesses of newspaper to absorb excess meltwater.

Place a large bowl on the top shelf of the fresh food compartment to catch water dripping from the drain hole above.

Put a large pot of hot steamy water into the freezer to start the frost melting.

Leave the freezer door open. Go away and do something else for an hour or two.

Come back. Throw out newspapers lining the freezer. *Gently* scrape and pry off any remaining frost with a *plastic*-coated pancake turner. Never use a sharp instrument to remove ice and don't poke. (Puncture the lining and you'll have to buy a new refrigerator.)

Mop up excess moisture with paper towels.

Wash freezer walls with a baking soda and warm water solution. Wipe dry.

Return food, which should still be partially frozen, to freezer.

Turn controls on.

When frost accumulations are heavy, more attention is needed, but the job can still be completed in a few hours. Follow the guidelines given above, but stay close by and keep replacing pots of hot water in the freezer while removing frost as it softens. When the job has been delayed too long, there may be ice hidden inside the lining of the freezer wall. If you've had trouble closing the freezer door because of frost, this is probably the case. It takes almost 24 hours to melt this hidden accumulation. Defrost normally to remove the surface ice and leave the freezer off overnight with a large bowl under the drip hole. Don't attempt to hold perishable foods for this length of time. Borrow space for perishables in a neighbor's refrigerator, if you can.

If your freezer seems to ice up too quickly,

check to see that doors close properly. Place a piece of paper between the door and the refrigerator and shut the door on it. If the paper pulls out easily, offering no resistance, the soft rubbery gasket that seals the door closed has worn out. Have the gasket replaced. Apply the same test to the gaskets lining the freezer door.

Stove

A modern range has been engineered to deliver even, easily adjustable heat. Its design furthers efficiency and its surfaces clean easily in comparison with stoves of the past. Get to know your own range. All models are somewhat different, and individual units develop heating quirks of their own that should be understood if you expect to cook with any degree of precision. Control knobs are rarely totally accurate indicators of temperature.

Select the right utensil for the job at hand. Pots made from heavy materials (cast aluminum, cast iron, thick enamel) are considered best for slow cooking. Their thick surfaces distribute and hold heat most evenly and are more amenable to gradient temperature changes than lighter materials. It is, for instance, often impossible to reduce a substance from a boil to a slow simmer in

132

a thin-metaled pot, which heats up quickly and brings liquids to a boil faster than a heavy pot; these are best for quick cooking jobs where subtle gradations in temperature are unnecessary. Lighter weight utensils are also much easier to lift and maneuver. To save fuel and speed up cooking, match the size of the pot to the diameter of the burner and the amount of food being prepared. A large pan takes longer to heat up and begin the cooking process and involves a bigger cleaning job than a small pan; a pot that is too small invites a messy "boil over." A pot that does not lie flat heats food unevenly. A snug lid limits the escape of moisture, which helps to keep the food from drying out or burning.

Electric burners heat more evenly than gas but are slower to warm up and take longer to cool down. To avoid overcooking on an electric burner, turn off the heat before the food is fully done. With gas, don't allow the flame to flare up and around the sides of the pot. On either a gas or an electric range, do not use a high temperature setting any longer than necessary. Highest heats are only to bring food quickly to cooking temperatures; they don't allow adequate control once heat builds up in the burner and cooking utensil.

To keep foods moist in oven cooking,

cover tightly and don't overcook. For a brown or crisp topping bake without a cover. When all-over browning is desired, use shallow-rimmed utensils or set food on a rack inside the utensil so it is completely exposed to hot air.

Casseroles cook best in the thick pots that have given them their name. A colored or dark exterior finish increases heat retention, which allows foods to be cooked at a lower temperature than that indicated in the recipe. Ovenproof plastic handles cannot take temperatures higher than 350° F. and should never be used under the broiler.

Try not to open the oven door while food is in preparation. This slows down the cooking process and may ruin heat-sensitive cakes, breads, and souffles. An oven thermometer is the most reliable method of establishing actual temperatures. A meat thermometer is the only sure way of knowing when a roast is done.

The design and insulation of modern ovens are greatly improved over those of the recent past. As a result, baking times suggested in many old recipes are inaccurate. When following any recipe for the first time or when preparing an old favorite in a new oven, set your kitchen timer to go off five minutes before the minimum time given in the recipe and check the cooking progress. For accurate baking, the oven should be preheated. Set the dial for the correct temperature and allow 15 minutes before placing food inside. Casseroles and roasts do not require preheating, but recipe times are based on a preheated oven so allow extra cooking time when you start cold.

To ensure that hot air circulates freely, do not overcrowd an oven. Allow space between pans and between utensils and the oven wall. Never set a pan directly on the oven floor. When using more than one rack, stagger utensils so the flow of air to the rack above or below is not blocked.

Broiling is a high-temperature, direct-heat cooking process. The closer food is placed to the heat source, the quicker it is done. For fastest results, or a crisp exterior, place the broiler close to the flame. For thicker pieces, move the broiler pan down a notch farther from the heat source, or the surface may burn before the inside is cooked. When using an electric broiler, leave the door ajar.

Warning note: Hot grease ignites easily and can catch fire without direct contact with the heat source. Don't try to save a wash-up job by covering the broiler grid with foil. If you use foil, puncture it, so grease can drain

135

through instead of collecting in hazardous pools near the heat source.

To make lightest work of the disagreeable job of cleaning a stove, clean as you go. Keep a soapy sponge handy when you cook and use a spoon rest (a sponge or saucer will do) for cooking utensils. Check the oven after using; if grease has splattered or a spill has occured, allow the oven to cool and wipe the interior with a damp sponge or paper towels. A plastic scrubber handles most fresh encrustations, and ammonia and hot water dissolve minor accumulations of grease. To make cleaning a broiling pan easier, remove from heat, sprinkle with dishwashing liquid, cover with damp paper towels, and let it sit till later.

The reflector pans that rim some stove-top burners are meant to shine. Clean as needed or use disposable foil designs if you can find a size that fits.

When a big stove cleaning job is inevitable, ammonia is a reliable cleaning agent. You can boost ammonia's cleaning power with Spic and Span or a heavy duty laundry detergent, or forgo the ammonia and use a bottled all-purpose cleaner. Wear rubber gloves and put all easily removed stove parts to soak in hot water and cleaning solution while you scrub as much of the stove as you can reach. When cleaning an electric range, watch where you probe; don't wet wires or burners. If wires are dirty, they just have to stay that way. Clean the burners of an electric range by turning heat on high for a minute or two until soil is burned away.

A favorite household hint: Put a large plastic garbage bag into the sink and put removable stove parts into it; pour in two cups of full-strength household ammonia; seal tight so fumes don't escape; let it remain overnight; next morning, slit bag and fill sink with hot water; add a handful of laundry detergent or Spic and Span; soak for 20 minutes; wash, rinse, and dry.

The only easy way to clean an oven is with a commercial oven cleaner. These cleaners contain corrosive chemicals. Wear goggles and rubber gloves and avoid spilling the cleaner on your skin; pump bottles allow for more control than aerosols. (If you do use an aerosol don't breathe the droplets). Follow product directions and precautions and don't use these cleaners for any part of the stove except the oven; especially avoid chrome. Rinse well after cleaning and heat oven before using to burn off any residue.

Follow manufacturer's directions for self- or continuous cleaning ovens.

Expedient note: An electric self-cleaning

oven is a great work saver. Continuous cleaning gas ovens rarely live up to expectations.

The Range Hood

This companion to the stove captures 75 percent of the small grease particles that would otherwise float around the house and settle down on walls and furniture. Install one as the manufacturer suggests; for most effectiveness, place the bottom of the hood as close to the top of the stove as you can without blocking your vision. Replace charcoal filters every six months and wash the metal filter in the dishwasher or use a brush and hot soapy water. Turn off electricity before washing hood and fan.

Safety at the stove: Do not use water to put out a grease fire; it spreads flames instead of dousing them. Turn off heat and stop the oxygen supply by closing the oven door or putting a lid on top of the pot. If fire continues, pour salt, flour, or baking soda directly onto the flames. Small dry-chemical fire extinguishers, designed just for kitchen use, are available. Direct the nozzle toward the base of the fire.

A few sensible precautions:
° A damp towel or pot holder intensifies

heat conduction, and a bad burn can result if one is used to lift a hot, heavy pot. Wet heat burns most quickly. Protect hands and face from steam.

° Don't let water steam from a pot directly into an electric outlet.

° Never use a match to check for a gas leak. If you suspect trouble, open the window and call the gas company.

° Teach children how to use a stove as soon as they are old enough to be trusted with a potentially dangerous assignment. Until then, don't leave them alone in the kitchen.

° Keep combustible objects out of the flames' reach. Be sure that curtains are not within a breeze-length of the stove top. Plastics, even without coming into direct contact with an open flame, may melt; aerosol cans can explode, and hot grease can ignite!

The Kitchen Sink

Your sink is the single most used piece of equipment in the kitchen. It is meant to take punishment and rarely lets you down if you take proper care of it. Don't let small solids slip into the drain with the dishwater. Pour or scrape grease into an empty can, milk container, or plastic bag for removal with the trash.

Strictly speaking, a swish with dishwashing liquid is all that's necessary to clean a sink, but a clean sink is not necessarily a sparkling one. For more of a gleam, scour once a week or twice a month with Bon Ami, the least abrasive of the scouring powders. (Don't use any scouring powder on stainless steel. Dishwashing liquid alone should do the trick, but if more help seems needed, use baking soda.) To brighten *white* porcelain, fill the sink with water, add a cup of chlorine bleach, and let sit for an hour. Avoid bleaching colored porcelain; white vinegar or lemon juice sometimes removes stains. Let it sit on the stain for half an hour or so.

For slow-moving drains: Pour a cup of salt, or a cup of vinegar, or a cup of baking soda, or a cup of Spic and Span down the drain; add a quart of boiling water; cover drain and wait an hour. If matters haven't improved, repeat.

A plunger, also known as a plumber's helper, nearly always handles a clogged drain. (Those meant to be used on a sink look like a rubber ball cut in half. The ones with rounded bottoms are for clogged toilets.) To use: Stuff rags into overflow outlets and auxiliary drains that share the same blocked pipes, such as the garbage disposal opening or the other drain of a twin sink. The plunger head must be large enough to cover the drain outlet. If the sink is empty, add enough water to cover the plunger head. Slide the head over the drain hole. Pump up and down hard and fast a dozen times. Jerk the plunger away suddenly. If water drains, the clog is removed. If it doesn't, try again. If the plunger is able to do the job, it usually works within five attempts. Follow by running very hot water in the sink. Should the clog persist, check a home repair book (see Bibliography) or call the plumber; pay careful attention to what the plumber does so you can take care of the drain yourself next time.

Commercial drain cleaners are not recommended; if you decide to try one, follow *all* package precautions. Do not use a commercial cleaner on a totally clogged sink. If the chemicals do not work, you or the plumber will have to contend with pipes and a sink filled with highly caustic liquid.

DISHWASHING AND KITCHEN MAINTENANCE

Dishwashing can, like so much else, be simplified with proper equipment, especially with an electric dishwasher. Everybody may not have one of these, but I certainly hope *you* do. These machines make much lighter work while freeing up sink and counter top space. The abilities of electric dishwashers vary greatly. Some do practically everything except carry the dishes from the table. Others demand a good deal of preparatory dish scraping and rinsing. Experiment with yours until you learn its strengths and limitations and establish a firm unloading routine.

If you have trouble with spotting of glasses and the like, try a different dishwashing product that may be better formulated to dissolve the minerals in your water. If this doesn't do the trick, try a rinsing agent such as Jet Dry. A dishwasher's performance depends primarily on really hot water, so avoid running the machine when your hot water tank is low. All products formulated for electric dishwashers clean without making suds. Any other type of detergent is guaranteed to bubble onto the kitchen floor in a truly dramatic fashion.

It gets very hot inside a dishwasher and dishwasher detergent is one of the harshest formulas in your cleaning arsenal. Don't risk fine crystal or tableware. Be especially careful of antiques. Untempered plastics and wood can't withstand the deluge of hot water and high drying heat. Sharp knives lose their edge, gilded china its gleam. Decals and hand-painted designs come off. Aluminum may discolor. Iron rusts. Nonstick surfaces lose their easy-clean characteristics. Don't rest sterling silver and aluminum next to each other; a chemical reaction can take place that will stain the silver.

Safety note: Dishwasher detergents are very toxic. Keep them away from crawling kids, who like their taste.

The drying process draws the most electricity. To save on utility bills, turn off the machine before it starts to dry, open the door, and let the dishes dry themselves.

There is absolutely no need to clean the inside of a dishwasher. Clean the outside when appropriate just as you would any other appliance.

When washing dishes by hand, establish a routine to speed up the task. Try to direct traffic so you work in one direction from start to finish.

° Keep liquid dishwashing detergent in a squeeze bottle by the sink, diluted half-water and half-product, and use it for spot surface cleaning as well as dishwashing. A splash of vinegar in the dishwater helps to cut grease.

° Hot water kills germs and get dishes

clean with less effort. Protect your hands with rubber gloves and work with the hottest water you can stand. However, don't use very hot water on plastics and never slip a cold glass into a hot sink. Use cold water to prerinse anything containing remnants of milk, potatoes, cereal, pasta, or eggs as heat causes these substances to adhere to dishes.

° Wash cleanest things first. When suds lose their oomph, drain the sink and start again. The fastest way to clean a sink full of dishes: Use a steel wool soap pad and work under hot running water, washing and rinsing as you go. (Not recommended for grandma's best dishes.)

° Never force your hand into a narrow glass. Use a long-handled brush.

° To clean a pot easily, fill it with water, add a squirt of detergent and put it to simmer on top of the stove. If the pot has burned-on food, add a few tablespoons of baking soda and simmer for 20 minutes. The only way to clean a badly burned pot is with a strong arm and steel wool.

° The discoloration that sometimes appears on aluminum cookware when certain foods are cooked in it, or after it has been exposed to a strong cleaning substance, is cosmetic. It does not mean the pot is unsafe for future use.

° When there's no time to wash, soak dishes. Restaurateurs recommend cold water; it softens many foods and congeals grease onto the plate instead of dissolving it in the water to cover every item being soaked. When you're ready to wash the dishes, drain the cold water and run in hot.

° When you are having difficulty staying on top of dishwashing, cut down on the dishes used. Put everything out of reach except for the essentials. Leave one dinner plate, one cereal bowl, one glass, one cup, and so on, accessible for every house member. Ask everyone to be responsible for washing his or her own after each meal and rotate the washing of pots and serving utensils. This is much more pleasant than using paper plates and almost as easy.

Work surfaces in the kitchen should be wiped with a sudsy sponge as part of your nightly dishwashing routines. Soap or detergent kills most household bacteria and leaves behind an alkaline pH in which germs do not thrive. Wooden counter tops and cutting boards may need special attention (see page 107).

Sweep the floor when kitchen activities are through for the day. If necessary, damp mop with plain water, or water and ammonia. An absorbent washable throw rug, with a nonskid backing, placed in front of the sink, is a good idea.

Lightly clean the external surfaces of your kitchen appliances and cabinets once a week. A mixture of 1 cup of water, 1 tablespoon of nonsudsing ammonia, and $\frac{1}{2}$ tablespoon of Spic and Span, kept in a spray bottle seems to be gentle on surfaces. (Don't mix with chlorine bleach.) Unplug small appliances before cleaning. To postpone cleaning small appliances, cover with decorative machine-washable, no-iron cloths. Cut them to fit and use pinking shears so you won't have to hem the edges.

Grease deposits on the walls around the stove are soon hardened by cooking heat, which makes for heavy cleaning. Before they accumulate, let a pot of water steam until the walls are moist; wipe dry with paper towels. When more cleaning is called for, let the steam do its job and wash with the mixture mentioned above. Work your way up to avoid drip stains.

A sponge mop can be used to clean cabinet doors and ceilings. Wrap a towel around the mop head to dry.

Your garbage pail will stay fresher longer if you use plastic garbage bags. Should you prefer paper, use a plastic bag to line the pail and change it as needed. Any cleanser will clean the pail well enough. It's not necessary to disinfect.

THE WELL-OUTFITTED KITCHEN

Culinary effort is much more effective, more pleasant, and much easier with the right tools. The following inventory will see you through most of the recipes in a standard cookbook. Gourmet cooks and frequent bakers may want to invest in specialty equipment, but, as a general rule, it is not necessary to spend a lot of money on individual kitchen items. Medium-priced, standard brand kitchenware serves well for most purposes and lasts for years. There are many tools available other than those listed here. Keep an eye out for those that will make your chores easier or give you better results. Remember, a tool is only worth owning if you love it or use it. Otherwise, it's a space-stealing gadget.

Here are the implements you are likely to need:
A 10″ or 12″ chef's or butcher's knife for slicing, carving, or chopping. A blade made from stainless steel with a high carbon content holds its edge better than pure stainless and doesn't discolor like carbon.

A small paring knife.

A 6″ serrated knife for slicing bread, soft fruits and vegetables, and cheeses.

A long-handled tubular knife sharpener (called a steel). Electric and mechanical models tend to ruin a knife blade; flint designs are more difficult to manipulate.

A long-handled sharp-tined fork for carving.

A hardwood cutting board at least 1″ thick provides a cutting and chopping surface. Plastic boards clean easily and don't accumulate scratches, but knives stay sharper and are less likely to slip on wood.

Poultry shears.

Scissors.

Two swivel-bladed vegetable peelers (one for the person who helps with the holiday potatoes).

A plastic-handled manual can opener is more reliable than the all-metal designs. Electric models are most convenient but look for a design that is easy to clean.

A square four-sided grater is most versatile. Metal stays sharp longer than plastic. For easier cleaning, brush with oil before using.

All cutting tools stay sharp longer when they are hand washed and well dried soon after use. Store so that the blades are protected from nicks and hands are protected from blades. Slotted wooden knife holders, which accommodate standard knife sizes, are readily available. Magnetic strips that hang on the wall are another alternative.

A colander with feet will stand by itself in the sink, leaving hands free to pour the pasta or sort through the berries. Larger sizes are most versatile; stainless steel cleans easier than plastic.

A mesh sieve with a long handle purees cooked fruits and vegetables and can also be used to sift flour and drain small quantities of cooked vegetables.

A wire whisk for delicate beating and stirring jobs.

A portable electric mixer for quick mixing batters or mashing potatoes.

A rubber spatula for folding and scraping the last bit from the bowl.

Several sizes of mixing bowls are helpful. A set of nesting stainless steel bowls gives a good range of sizes. Plastic is lightweight but scratches easily; taste-sensitive cooks believe it imparts taste to foods.

A flour sifter that incorporates a measuring cup.

A Pyrex measuring cup for liquid ingredients.

A set of graduated measuring cups for dry ingredients.

A set of measuring spoons. (Cups, tablespoons, and teaspoons designed for the table are not standard in size. Avoid using them as measures.)

A large salad bowl. Wooden bowls are not dishwasherproof and can't be soaked in the sink. Glass is easy to clean and shows off the salad.

A bottle opener.

An apron with large pockets made from bleachproof fabric such as white canvas.

When it comes to pots and pans the biggest problem is choosing from the vast array in the store. A few guidelines: Select well-balanced pots that do not tip or rock when placed on a flat surface. Flat-bottomed, straight-sided utensils with snug covers retain heat best. Knobs and handles should be securely attached, comfortable in the hand, and heat resistant. Ovenproof handles and knobs increase versatility. Matched sets are less expensive than pieces sold separately but almost always contain pieces that go unused. A selection of unmatched pieces chosen to meet your needs may be a better bet.

When buying, ask for assurances that a

utensil conducts heat evenly, does not impart taste to food, and resists warping. Stainless steel is attractive and easiest to clean, but it is not a good conductor of heat. Aluminum conducts heat quickly and evenly but discolors easily and can affect the taste of goods that contain acid, such as tomato sauce. As a compromise measure, stovetop stainless steel utensils are often made with an aluminum bottom.

Pots with nonstick interiors are a less-work option, but care must be taken to avoid scratching the nonstick surface; once food burns onto one of these easy-clean surfaces it becomes hard to clean. SilverStone is currently the smoothest and toughest of the nonstick surfaces.

Lightweight enamel chips easily. Copper is an excellent heat conductor, but pots with copper bottoms are hard to clean. Corningware is easy to clean, absorbs and holds heat well, and does not break as easily as glass. It has the further advantage of being able to travel from the freezer to the oven or top of the stove and to the table. Tempered glass tends to develop hot spots on top of the stove and should not be used for cooking vegetables, because light-sensitive nutrients will be destroyed during the cooking process.

For slow cooking of sauces and stews a

heavy pot is advised. Cast iron is excellent and reasonable in cost but must be washed by hand and dried well to prevent rust. It also requires an occasional reseasoning with oil. Heavy enamelware that features enamel over a steel or iron core is very easy to clean and goes attractively from stove to table.

Persistent rumors abound that one or another of the materials used in the manufacture of cookware is unsafe. According to the Food and Drug Administration (FDA) these rumors are unfounded; all commonly used materials are safe for cooking. According to Adelle Davis, who was one of the first to cast doubt on the assurances of the FDA, utensils made from stainless steel are potentially dangerous. She approved of aluminum, but some alternate-culture food authorities question its long-term effects, while others worry about non-stick interiors. If this is a concern of yours, choose enamel, porcelain, tempered glass, iron, or Corningware. Handmade pottery is a potential risk because toxic substances, which may be unknowingly contained in their glaze, can contaminate food. Copper utensils should not come into contact with food unless they are lined with tin.

Useful pots, pans, and stove-related accessories include:

Two saucepans with lids. Useful sizes are $1\frac{1}{2}$, $2\frac{1}{2}$, or 3 quarts.

A small pan (2–3 cup capacity) for melting butter or heating milk. Enamel is easier to clean than metal.

A 10"–12" skillet is a kitchen essential. Sloping sides make it easier to manipulate foods with a fork or pancake turner. A lid, while not necessary, can be helpful.

A small skillet (6"–7") for little jobs such as sauteing one onion.

A large pot (6–8 quarts or more) for proper pasta cooking and the preparation of large quantities of vegetables. Since this is only going to be used to boil water, the dime-store version is fine.

A 5-quart Dutch oven made from cast iron or heavy enamel for slow stove-top cooking and large casseroles. This should have ovenproof handles and a snug fitting cover.

A medium-sized lidded casserole (about 2 quarts).

A smaller lidded casserole for baked vegetables and desserts.

A large uncovered roasting pan with wire rack for the big roast or turkey. The broiler pan that comes with the stove is perfectly adequate for chicken and small roasts.

A tea kettle.

A folding vegetable steamer that fits inside a saucepan or a pot designed especially for steaming.

A wok for speedy, healthful stir-frying. With a special insert, a wok can also be used as a food steamer.

A slotted pancake turner allows you to drain off oil as you lift.

A large metal spoon with holes in the bowl drains liquid back into the pot.

A long-handled wooden spoon with a slightly pointed bowl can get down into the corners of a pot.

A pair of metal tongs with looped handles makes it easy to remove a strand of pasta for testing or to lift something like corn or asparagus from the water.

A long-handled ladle for spooning out soups and stews.

A windup timer with a loud buzz.

An oven thermometer. If your stove is beyond middle age, the markings on the control dial are probably not reliable.

A meat thermometer.

A long shish kebab skewer conveniently holds a string of potatoes, onions, or beets and helps to speed up their baking.

Several thick, flame-resistant pot holders.

Those with mitts at either end protect the body when lifting large pots.

The amount of baking done in any household varies greatly. The following general guidelines will do for the occasional cake, pie, or batch of holiday cookies. Specialty cookbooks offer more advanced suggestions.

For cake, quick breads, and cookies choose bright or light-colored pans. Dark or discolored utensils are too heat absorbing and cause overbrowning. Use glass or dull-surfaced pie plates for crisper crust. Dark-colored pans are often recommended for bread making. Save baking gear for baking; don't use it on top of the stove or for casserole cooking.

One 9"×13" oblong or two 8" round cake pans will meet most cake recipe and mix requirements. A nonstick interior is helpful.

Pie pans come in various sizes, but many recipes call for a 9" diameter.

Two cookie tins with rimless sides.

A wire cooling rack.

Small Appliances

A few small appliances – the electric mixer, blender, and toaster – are now considered indispensable. Other appliances have proved their value and should be considered efficiency improvers. Before making a purchase, ask yourself, "Will this do a better or faster job than the method I am now using? Will it make the job more pleasant? Will I *actually* use it?" You might borrow the appliance under consideration for a week or two from a friend so you can see if you are willing to adjust your routines to the new device. One problem with new appliances – even those that are genuine work and time savers – is that it takes a certain amount of determination to incorporate new methods into set routines. Old habits die hard.

Decide where the appliance will be kept before you buy it. Remember, if you cannot make convenient space for something it is much less likely to be used on a regular basis. Consider, too, the appliance's cleaning requirements. Because it is much easier to wash a knife and a chopping block than the parts of a food processor, most of us will not use the processor for a small job like chopping a few onions. When Chinese cuisine is a house specialty, however, the work of cleaning the complex device is a snap in comparison to dicing and slicing all those vegetables.

When selecting any electrical appliance, buy one that carries the Underwriters'

Laboratory Seal and be sure your home wiring is adequate. Look for durable, easy-to-clean surfaces, with no crevices or sharp corners. Detachable parts should be simple to remove and replace, and on/off switches and controls conveniently placed and easy to operate. Before buying, check the care-use manual to ascertain that your machine will do all that you expect it to and, if it's not quite what you want, investigate other models.

The *electric mixer* is the quickest way to accomplish any number of tasks from beating up a cake mix to mashing potatoes. The standing model with its hand-freeing, built-in base and powerful motor is the choice of serious cooks. The smaller portable is easy to store and will give adequate service for years.

The *blender* is an invaluable tool that blends, grates, crumbs, liquifies, minces, and purees. It is also trim enough to sit easily on even the smallest counter top, and it takes very little effort to clean. If you don't have a blender, get one. It will simplify your cooking routines and help you prepare the salt-free soups, high-energy drinks, and low-calorie salad dressings that are the new mainstay of quick, nutritious cooking. Choose a quality tool with a strong motor, several speeds, and a responsive on/off switch. Glass containers stay attractive longer than plastic and do not retain food odors, but they do break when dropped on the floor. To clean: Fill container half full with warm water and add a splash of dishwashing liquid. Turn blender on to low speed. Rinse and allow to dry upside down on the counter.

What kitchen is complete without a *toaster?* The only question is whether to have a simple model or the multipurpose *toaster oven.* The smaller pop-up toaster makes better toast faster than an oven design, but it won't bake a potato or heat a frozen pot pie. When using a pop-up toaster, remember that the old rule, "Never stick anything inside a toaster except for a piece of bread," still holds. Always unplug a toaster before probing inside.

Because the toaster oven heats faster than a conventional oven, it is especially useful where small quantities of food are often wanted in a hurry. Many households, however, do not use the additional features often enough to justify the higher purchase price or the extra counter space. If you decide on a toaster oven, purchase one that gives the most options and read the booklet that comes with the appliance so you will know its full helpful potential.

None of the following is essential, but any one of them can be valuable.

The *electric fry pan*. Its primary advantages are its large size, domed lid, and controlled heat that allow the easy cooking of stew or fricassee like one-dish meals. It slow simmers beautifully and is a favorite of the cook who prefers to put the fixings together, set a switch, and come back later to find a cooked meal. Some models can bake, roast, and broil as well. Look for large capacity, a lid that has a sliding vent to let steam escape, and detachable controls that allow the pan to be submerged in water for cleaning.

The *crock pot* is another favorite that allows a cook to toss together a few ingredients in the morning and come back to a tasty healthful meal when the day is done. Look for a design with a cooking insert that lifts out easily for cleaning.

The *rice cooker* is fast gaining in popularity among the expedient kitchen set. Its name belies its usefulness, and smart manufacturers are beginning to call it what it is: an electric steam cooker. This appliance can be used to make perfect rice, soup, and stews; steam vegetables, hotdogs, and shellfish; heat leftovers; freshen stale bread and rolls; and boil water, eggs and spaghetti. The rice cooker is usually a Japanese import, so directions are not always adapted to occidental uses. To get the full value from this versatile device a bit of intelligent trial and error is in order; *Consumer Reports* (July 1981) feels that experimentation is worth the results. Look for a model with a large capacity and a holding device for keeping foods warm. Rice can be held for as long as an hour without drying out.

The *food processor* is of limited value in kitchens where simple food is the order of the day. The old-fashioned blender, which is unobtrusive on the counter and easy to clean, actually performs many similar jobs. However, the food processor can do more – it chops meat, shreds cabbage, slices zucchini, and kneads dough. It is at its best when used for large, tedious jobs that would take hours of hand work or frequent refilling of the blender. Those who bake bread, and cooks who specialize in French, Oriental, or vegetarian cuisine find it invaluable; many others find it a helpful addition. The more expensive models give better long-term service. Cutting blades hold up longer and motors are better at grinding and kneading chores. For sometime use, the cheaper models are fine.

All-in-one-machines are appliances that use one motor to power a food processor, blender, and standing mixer. Most also offer optional extras such as an electric can opener, citrus or vegetable juicer, or coffee mill. These expensive machines are very space-efficient devices that provide a ready food preparation center and the luxury of owning appliances that one might ordinarily pass over because of infrequency of use. To consider: All-in-one-machines of any kind are tools of compromise, with versatility the essential element. To achieve this, best performance in any one area is often sacrificed. If what you want is a super blender, don't settle for a good enough blender just because you get a mixer in the same package.

Many cooks find a *microwave oven* indispensable. It's especially valuable to those who prepare their own TV dinners by cooking large quantities in advance and freezing portions.

This form of cookery uses microwaves to vibrate the moisture molecules in food. The vibration causes heat, which in turn cooks. It's a speedy process in which nothing gets hot except the food being cooked. Raw vegetables can be cooked right in their plastic storage bags. Cocoa can be heated in the same cup from which it will be drunk.

However, there are some problems. Foods do not brown on the surface and some, such as leg of lamb, take almost as long to cook as they would in a conventional oven. Foods can also cook unevenly depending on their density and distribution of water. Many new model microwave ovens have special controls that improve all-over performance. They are also built with safeguards that practically eliminate the possibility that microwaves will leak from the oven into the home environment, a common fear among many householders. Research indicates that there is no health risk involved with microwave cookery so long as directions are followed *and* the protective seal remains intact. *Exception:* People wearing pace-makers should avoid microwaves.

Seven

A Shorter Wash Day

For many people, especially those who don't own their own washing machines, getting the laundry done is the most troublesome household job. To reduce the wash load, buy sensibly, cultivate neatness, and eliminate as many cloth extras as possible from the home scene. All this will help. But the real key to success is to avoid falling behind. Do laundry a bit at a time, schedule a regular wash day, send it all out, but get it done promptly. Delay means bigger piles and entrenched soil is much, much harder to remove than fresh.

A shorter wash day begins at the stores where you buy your clothing and household goods. Try not to purchase simply in terms of an article's style value. Consider the cost of its upkeep as well – whether in dry-cleaning bills or the costs to you in time-and-effort of laundering and ironing. Learn to read labels and familiarize yourself with the care requirements of different fibers. Some fabrics, such as no-iron cotton or blends of polyester and cotton or wool, are much easier to maintain than others. Consider colors. When you live in a city that suffers from air pollution, pastels can mean one-time use only.

Clothing upkeep deserves special consideration. A simple reality that most of us overlook is that clothing is not a one-time investment. A dress that costs three dollars to be dry-cleaned and has to be dry-cleaned frequently can easily double its cost before a year has passed. If it takes you 20 minutes to hand wash and iron that same dress and you do this only 50 times before you pass it on to your favorite charity, you have given it $16\frac{1}{2}$ hours of your life. You really have to like that garment an awful lot to make it worth owning.

Examine the clothes you already possess. If you have one item that always seems to be in your closet ready to be worn, analyze its virtues. Search out others that share whatever remarkable attributes that garment has; is it an easy shape that does not invite creases or a material that rejects wrinkles, a fabric that seems to stay clean forever, or an article that comes out of the washing machine ready to be worn? Workhorse items such as these have far more value than the nifty-looking somethings that are always at the cleaners, in the bottom of the to-be-done basket, or not fresh when you really need them. The trick is to manage to combine good looks with the functional qualities that make your life easier.

As a general rule, men's clothing is much more maintenance-free than women's. But men, too, should be aware of the pitfalls of style-determined buying. Normally, an all-cotton designer's shirt requires much more from the wearer and from an iron than an everyman's permanent press. Parents should not get carried away when buying clothing for children. Ruffles are fine, as long as they are genuinely drip-dry, but little girls who hanker after the starched look should be encouraged to appreciate the charms of a good pair of jeans and a T-shirt. (When and if you have teenagers, we assume they will be doing their own wash.)

Learn how to take care of clothing. Every time you wash or dry-clean a cloth item, you shorten its life. Chemicals (and even soap is a chemical) damage the fibers from which the fabric is made. The processes of cleaning, washing, and tumble drying put additional stress on seams and fabric. You can cut down on the number of cleanings by instilling a few old-fashioned habits into the daily routine.

FIBER CHARACTERISTICS

	Acetate	Acrylic	Aramid	Metallic	Modacrylic	Nylon	Olefin	Polyester	Rayon	Saran	Spandex	Triacetate	Vinyon
Absorbent									√				
Colorfast		√		√		√	√	√	√	√		√	
Easy to dye	√	√				√			√			√	
Easy to launder		√	√	√		√	√	√	√		√	√	
Easy to iron		√				√	√	√				√	
Elastic						√					√		
Exceptional durability		√	√			√	√	√		√			
Flame resistant			√		√					√			
Good drapability	√	√				√			√			√	
Good shape retention		√				√	√	√			√	√	
Quick drying		√	√			√	√	√			√	√	
Resilient		√	√			√	√	√					
Resistant to:													
abrasion		√				√	√	√					
chemicals		√	√		√	√	√	√		√			
moth	√	√	√	√	√	√	√	√	√	√	√	√	√
mildew	√	√	√	√	√	√	√	√		√	√	√	√
oil and grease		√	√			√				√			
pilling	√								√			√	
stretching			√					√					

	Acetate	Acrylic	Aramid	Metallic	Modacrylic	Nylon	Olefin	Polyester	Rayon	Saran	Spandex	Triacetate	Vinyon
Resistant to:													
soil			√				√						
shrinking		√	√	√		√		√			√	√	
weather		√		√	√		√	√	√	√			
Soft	√	√			√				√				
Strong			√			√	√	√		√			
Warm		√			√	√		√					
Wide color range	√	√			√	√		√	√			√	
Wrinkle resistant		√						√			√	√	

Source: Man-Made Fiber Producers Association, Inc.

Natural fibers (cotton, linen, silk, wool) have their own well-known and attractive characteristics. The drawback is that they almost always require more upkeep time. Blends of natural and synthetic fibers often offer the best qualities of both. A blend must contain at least 25 percent of any one fiber in order to retain its special characteristics. *Exception:* A content of 2 percent Spandex and 15 percent nylon is adequate.

Brush (or at least shake out) clothing after wearing. Hang your clothes up immediately after taking them off. Use a proper hanger. Those supplied by the dry cleaner are meant for temporary use only. Padded or rounded plastic hangers mean fewer crease marks. If your closets are so full that there is little air movement, put the garment on a hanger and let it air for the night outside the closet door. Do timely spot cleaning (see Stain Prevention). Learn to eat neat. And rely on the deodorant that's best for you.

Don't be too quick with an iron. Pressing can permanently set a stain. An old traveling salesman's trick: Hang a wrinkled article of clothing in the bathroom; turn on the hot water to fill the room with steam; turn off the water; seal the bottom of the bathroom door with a rolled-up towel; leave the garment for 20 minutes. The steam will almost always remove the wrinkles, but allow the garment to dry before hanging it in a closed closet.

Consider the virtues of a double wardrobe – one for public, the other for private life. This is not a matter of tightwad economics (although if our economy continues on its peculiar path, it may come to this) but rather making sure that image-projecting clothing is available when needed, even if the week has been too hectic to allow for serious laundry. Private-sector clothing should be no-worry, easy stuff that can be thrown into the washer and put away clean and wearable. It should be comfortable and becoming and all those nice things, too. Removing "good" clothing immediately on walking in the door and slipping into an at-home outfit also helps one to make the psychological shift from work to home, but its primary advantage is simply saving the dress or shirt for another day. Just sitting around watching TV can finish off an outfit that otherwise could have made it one more time.

All this, of course, should not be pushed to the point of silliness. The eye (and the nose) are your best determination of when it is definitely time to clean an item. You may be surprised, though, by how long the inevitable can be postponed.

WASH DAY

Not so long ago, simply getting laundry clean enough was a major accomplishment. Today with modern detergents, fabrics, and washing machines getting the stuff clean is a snap. The question has become, "Does it look clean?" Misguided wash day efforts can result in a dingy, stained, faded, wrinkled product, and it's rarely the detergent, machine, or fabric that's at fault. The problem is poor or out-of-date technique. Many of us still do laundry the way our grandmothers did. Make note. The rules have changed. The standby fabrics of old, which could stand up to remedial bleaching and hot, hot water have been largely replaced with permanent press and synthetics, which prefer gentler treatment. Modern detergents and washing machines do not perform their wizardly without help. To get worthwhile results, you have to know what you're doing.

Which Laundry Products?

Detergents: Unless you live in a soft water area (or in an area where the use of detergent is not allowed), don't attempt to do laundry with soap. Getting fabrics free of the curds that result when minerals and soap combine in hard water is more of an operation than anyone needs. Choose an all-purpose laundry detergent for everything except your most delicate things. Liquid dishwashing detergent is recommended for hand washables. Detergents containing phosphates give best results, but these cause cesspools to fill up faster and are serious water polluters. Many locales have banned their use and many consumers prefer to avoid them even when they are available. Labels clearly state whether a product contains phosphates. Our guidelines are for nonphosphate detergents. If you launder with soap powder, follow product directions meticulously.

It is difficult to suggest any one product because detergent formulas are constantly being modified. Besides, the same brand name (and package) is used for both phosphate and nonphosphate product versions; although the name remains the same, the formula can vary from one part of the country to the other, depending on whether phosphates are allowed. As far as I can determine all brand name products will deliver as long as the manufacturer's directions are followed. No-name, also called generic, and store brands don't seem to be as effective. I recommend choosing a liquid because liquids can be added to the machine at any time, *whereas powders must first be dissolved in wash water before the laundry is added* to ensure a clean wash and to prevent powdery residue. Also liquids can be applied directly to soil for easy pre-treatment, but powders must first be mixed with water to make a paste. Powders also produce a small amount of clinging film, similiar to soap curd.

Try a few products and see which gives you the best results. The degree of hard water and your particular laundry problems may make a difference. Whenever you use a new product, read its label to find out how much to use. Correct measurements are important and specifications differ from product to product. If you have very soft water, or use a front-loading machine, choose a low-sudsing detergent.

All modern detergents are potent chemical mixes and highly toxic when ingested, especially to children. Sometimes an allergic reaction, in the form of a rash or chronic itch, may develop. Try changing detergents and brush up on your laundry techniques to ensure thorough rinsing. Occasionally, after the regular washing is complete, run the laundry through the entire wash/rinse cycle again, *omitting detergent*. This trick sometimes brightens dull looking laundry as well.

Prewash treatments: Normally, regular laundry detergent does fine as a presoak or spot cleaner. A liquid detergent is the handiest, especially when kept in a small squirt bottle. Some people prefer the specially formulated pretreatment products, such as Shout. Arm & Hammer Detergent Booster is a good presoak for those who deal with unusually heavy soil.

Bleaches: When it's safe to use it, chlorine bleach removes or diminishes some stains and brightens white and colorfast fabrics. It's hard on fibers, however, and it contributes to colors' fading. Using it every time, even on those fabrics that can withstand its harsh effects, is not recommended. Save it for stain removal or as a last-ditch attempt to restore dingy looking things. With proper laundering techniques, there may be no need to bleach at all.

Never use bleach on wool, silk, acetate, elastic, spandex, or anything that bears a label stating "no chlorine bleach." Even white cottons, which are generally considered bleachproof, can be discolored if they have a resin finish. If there's iron in the wash water, it will react with bleach to turn things yellow. (Bleach makes rust stains worse. To remove rust, use Rit color remover on whites; try lemon juice or a rust remover purchased at a hardware store on colored fabrics.)

To use chlorine bleach, follow package directions carefully. *Never, ever, ever* mix it with anything but laundry or liquid dishwashing detergent (see p. 242). To give the most protection to fibers and to prevent white spots on colors, always dilute liquid bleach before adding it to the wash; never pour full strength bleach directly onto a fabric in an attempt to remove a stain. Powdered chlorine bleaches do not have to be diluted because they do not begin to work until mixed with water, but they are not quite as effective as the liquids.

Don't confuse powdered oxygen bleaches, such as Clorex 2 or Snowy, with chlorine bleaches, whether powder or liquid. These have a totally different chemical makeup and are meant to be used regularly as a preventive measure. They are of little use once a stain has set or a fabric grayed. They are nowhere near as effective as chlorine bleach, but they can be used without hesitation so long as the fabric label does not read *no bleach* (as opposed to no chlorine bleach) and package directions are followed. Those that list persulfate as the main ingredient are most effective. People who deal with badly soiled white or light-colored uniforms (and are tired of replacing them every six months when chlorine bleach disintegrates the fabric) or athletes whose bras or athletic supporters get discolored by body oils and perspiration may find them especially useful. In my opinion, most of us really don't need them.

Water softeners: Every all-purpose laundry detergent contains water softeners. Few of us need to add more. But when water is exceptionally hard (if you reside in an area with really hard water, you know it by the mineral stains in your toilet bowl or the soap curd in the bathtub), water softener should be added to wash water. Phosphate-based softeners do by far the best, most effective job. If you choose not to use one, or if they are not available in your area, Arm and

Hammer Detergent Booster is a reliable product.

Fabric softeners: Fabric softeners reduce lint and static cling and help to cut down on ironing chores. Many people find, however, that liquids leave a lintlike substance or greasy coating on fabric. When you use such a product follow directions and don't use too much! If you're dissatisfied with results, discontinue its use. One-half cup of Borax used instead of softener will sweeten the wash and leave fibers clean. Treated "paper" sheets create a fuzzy substance that accumulates in the air vents of a dryer, which slows down the process. They can also leave fabrics feeling a bit "greasy." However, such products really are helpful, and are less likely to cause problems than liquids. A compromise measure: Use half a sheet once or twice a month. Enough residue will remain in your dryer to give you most of the benefits without the side effects. Don't confuse fabric softeners with water softeners. They are two entirely different products.

Wash Day Techniques
   ° Don't let laundry pile up for more than a week. Fresh soils are easily cleaned. Old ones settle in, sometimes forever. Some households prefer to do wash a little at a

time. Most elect for a weekly wash day (or night).

° Separate whites and light-colored articles from darks. Identify shrinkables and anything that runs and be sure not to wash them in hot water. Empty pockets. Close zippers. Turn dark clothing inside out to avoid lint.

° Check for spots and heavy soil; dampen fabric and work liquid laundry detergent, or a pretreatment product, into the offending mark. Before washing, use plain cold water to remove protein-based stains (such as blood, egg, and milk) and fruit stains. Presoaking may be necessary (see Stain Prevention). Wash these in warm, not hot, water.

° Use warm water in general. Warm water is easier on fabrics and colors than hot and less likely to "cook" in stains or cause shrinkage. Because most detergents do their best work at higher temperatures, reserve cold water for light soil or special problems. (Water temperatures lower than 80° F. are not recommended for laundry.)

° Wash very dirty things, like gardening clothes or children's play clothes, in hot water if the fabric is shrinkproof and colorfast. (To avoid unpleasant surprises, check fabric-care labels and tags.) Hot water is best for greasy soil (such as vegetable or machine oil) but should not be used when there is starch or protein involved; warm water only for gravy or cream sauce. No-nonsense whites, such as underwear or socks, also do well in hot water, unless heavy perspiration is a problem. In this case, the use of warm water will help prevent yellowing.

° If you have the opportunity, use the washing machine to presoak badly soiled articles. Load the machine as you normally do, and add detergent, but stop the wash cycle after it has agitated for a few minutes. Allow wash to soak for 15 minutes before continuing the wash cycle. Presoak badly stained items, such as blood- or urine-soaked sheets, in the same fashion but use plain cool water. Then add detergent and continue wash cycle. Check to see that stain is gone before placing things in dryer.

° Measure detergent according to package directions. Too little won't get fabrics clean. Too much won't rinse out but will settle back onto fibers. Use extra detergent when soil is especially heavy or when water is hard, but refer to the label for the correct amount.

° Don't overload the washing machine. Things must circulate freely in plenty of water to get clean of dirt and detergent. And overcrowding leads to wrinkles. A half-full machine is usually full enough. When in doubt, underload. If possible, mix large and small items together in the same machine. Place heavy items at the bottom and lighter things on top. Give bulky items, like bedspreads, a machine of their own, one per machine.

° Separate synthetics and permanent press from other fabrics and wash together in warm water but rinse in cold to prevent wrinkles. Keep the load on the small side but set machine for a large load.

° Wash and dry dark things separately. Even when the dyes no longer run, trace amounts of color may rub off and dull lighter colors. Darks and bright colors will stay fresh-looking longer if washed in cool water. By the same token, whites stay whiter if kept separate from colored things. Even pastels can shed color in a washing machine.

° Don't crowd the dryer. The rule of thumb is one washing machine load equals one dryer load. Clothes will dry faster with fewer wrinkles if you follow this advice. One no-iron approach to clothing maintenance recommends putting only a few things at a time into the dryer and pulling them out as soon as they are dry.

° Avoid overdrying. Too much heat sets

wrinkles, is hard on fibers, fades colors, and causes shrinkage. Stand by the dryer and pull things out when they are ready. Delicate or shrinkable items are best tumbled without heat or allowed to dry naturally.

° Fold laundry as you take it from the dryer or put it directly onto hangers. When time is crucial, pipe unfolded articles very loosely in the carrying basket. To erase wrinkles, try putting a wet towel (wrung out) and the wrinkled clothes back into the drier for 10 minutes.

° Never fold damp things or pack them tightly. This sets creases and causes a sour odor. Spread them loosely on a flat surface, such as a bed or table, to continue drying.

CLOTHING CARE LABELS' MEANINGS
MACHINE WASHABLE

When label reads:	It means:
Machine wash	Wash, bleach, dry, and press by any customary method including commercial laundering and dry-cleaning
Home launder only	Same as above but do not use commercial laundering
No chlorine bleach	Do not use chlorine bleach; oxygen bleach may be used
No bleach	Do not use any type of bleach
Cold wash, Cold rinse	Use cold water from tap or cold washing machine setting
Warm Wash, Warm rinse	Use warm water or warm washing machine setting

MACHINE WASHABLE

When label reads:	It means:
Hot wash	Use hot water or hot washing machine setting
No spin	Remove wash load before final machine spin cycle
Delicate cycle, Gentle cycle	Use appropriate machine setting otherwise wash by hand
Durable press cycle, Permanent press cycle	Use appropriate machine setting; otherwise use warm wash, cold rinse, and short spin cycle
Wash separately	Wash alone or with like colors

NON-MACHINE WASHING

When label reads:	It means:
Hand wash	Launder only by hand in lukewarm (hand comfortable) water; may be bleached; may be dry-cleaned
Hand wash only	Same as above, but do not dry clean
Hand was separately	Hand wash alone or with like colors
No bleach	Do not use bleach
Damp wipe	Surface clean with damp cloth or sponge

HOME DRYING

When label reads:	It means:
Tumble dry	Dry in tumble dryer at specified setting—high, medium, low, or no heat
Tumble dry, remove promptly	Same as above, but in absence of cool-down cycle remove at once when tumbling stops
Drip dry	Hang wet and allow to dry with hand shaping only

HOME DRYING

When label reads:	It means:
Line dry	Hang damp and allow to dry
No wring, no twist	Hang dry, drip dry, or dry flat only; handle to prevent wrinkles and distortion
Dry flat	Lay garment on flat surface
Block to dry	Maintain original size and shape while drying

IRONING OR PRESSING

When label reads:	It means:
Cool iron	Set iron at lowest setting
Warm iron	Set iron at medium setting
Hot iron	Set iron at hot setting
Do not iron	Do not iron or press with heat
Steam iron	Iron or press with steam
Iron damp	Dampen garment before ironing

MISCELLANEOUS

When label reads:	It means:
Dry-clean only	Garment should be dry-cleaned only, including self-service
Professionally dry-clean only	Do not use self-service dry-cleaning
No dry-clean	Use recommended care instructions; no dry-cleaning materials used

Source: American Apparel Manufacturers Association.

Public machines

You can usually tell someone who uses a public washing machine by the lifeless condition of their washables. This comes from jamming too many things into each machine to save change and to get the job done quickly. All coin-operated laundry rooms have peak-use periods. If you can't do the job some other time, pretreat heavy soil and spots before your arrival and don't give in to public pressure to double up in the washer or dryer to free machines for those waiting. The guidelines given under Wash Day Techniques can all be followed in coin-operated appliances. You can even presoak if the washer has a turn-off/turn switch. Public dryers are usually much too hot. Don't go away and come back later, but stay nearby and remove things as they dry.

Many people use commercial laundromats where wash is dropped off in the morning and picked up in the evening – clean and folded. These are a great convenience but you don't have much control once the laundry leaves your hands, so prepare in advance. Pretreat soil and spots, presort your machine loads into individual pillowcases or laundry bags. Again, avoid overcrowding. It's not worth the money saved. If the establishment manager is sympathetic, pin water temperature instructions onto each load.

Those who do not have private machines may well find it worthwhile to do more of their laundry by hand. Most synthetics and permanent press articles release soil easily. Instead of tossing a piece of clothing into the hamper at night, douse it up and down in detergent and water in the sink or bathtub; rinse thoroughly and let drip-dry (but not on metal hangers, which cause rust stains). Save the hard-to-wash stuff that can take the punishment (such as sheets, towels, and underwear) for the washing machine. A wash-as-you-go routine is much easier when the bathroom is outfitted with either a folding rack that fits inside the tub, or a permanently installed pull-out clothesline.

Many apartment dwellers cannot find the time to get to the public machines on a regular basis. If this is your problem, and especially if you have young children, consider buying an apartment-sized washer and dryer, which are somewhat compact in size and operate on normal household current. These are usually on wheels and hook up easily (and temporarily) to the kitchen or bathroom sink.

Stain Prevention

If you hold to a weekly laundry schedule, and pretreat as part of your regular routine, most stains will disappear in the wash. However, this is not always the case. Thrift shops are filled with things that should have come clean but didn't. There are dozens of methods designed to prevent such permanent discoloration; each is appropriate for one or another stain or fabric. Most people forgo them in favor of a few commonsense techniques.

If something is especially important to you, get to an expert *fast!* Your best bet is a *reliable* dry cleaner or hand laundry. One test of reliability: Point out the stain, indicate the article's value, but don't say anything about what caused it. If it's taken from you, no question asked, retrieve it immediately and try another establishment. *Expert* stain removal is based on knowledge of how stains, cleaning solvents, and fabrics interact. Don't pay for amateur work when you can do that yourself.

No matter what the circumstances, these two rules hold true:
(1) The longer you wait, the poorer the chances of removal, and (2) heat sets many stains, making it impossible to remove them. As dry-cleaning and professional laundering

involve heat, always call attention to even simple stains and say what caused them so they can be pretreated. Never put stained things into hot water or the clothes drier and don't iron them. Don't expect miracles. Some substances are almost impossible to remove, and some fabrics are more retentive than others. No stain removal tactic is foolproof.

Although the wrong treatment can sometimes set a stain, for everyday things it's usually worth taking a small risk to avoid the cost of professional laundering or dry-cleaning. As long as a relatively fresh stain is not exposed to heat, there's almost always a further action that can be taken. If simple remedial techniques don't handle the problem, you can then seek out the expert. To be on the safe side, don't assume that a stain is completely gone after pretreatment even if you can no longer see it. Launder in warm water, or alert the dry cleaner, in case trace amounts are lingering in the fibers.

This quick-action tactic works for most food-related stains (such as, milk, fruit, soft drinks, wine, alcohol, beer, coffee, tea, gravy, chocolate, blood, urine, fecal matter, vomit). It's safe for washable fabrics and when done properly usually loosens stains enough for normal laundering or cleaning processes to finish the job. Its secret is immediacy. As soon as the spill occurs, find a water faucet. Use cool water only. Hold the fabric inside out close to the faucet so water pressure can help to force the stain out of the fiber. Flush away as much as you can. If you can't remove a garment to give it a proper flooding, dab (don't rub) at the mark with a wet towel or napkin. Some fabrics (most often silk) will show a water mark until washed or cleaned. If a visible trace of the stain remains, one of the following techniques should do the trick for washable fabrics only. If these fail, bring the article to the dry cleaner for expert attention; and be sure to describe the measures you have taken.

Greasy Stains: This is only for pure oil or grease (vegetable oil, butter, and the like). If any other element is involved follow the steps suggested below for combination stains. *Exception:* This tactic usually works for makeup. Dampen fabric and rub in full strength liquid laundry detergent, working up suds. If the article is not to be laundered immediately, rinse with hot water. Launder normally. Should the stain persist after laundering, sponge on dry-cleaning fluid. Several applications may be needed, but let the fabric dry between applications. Some synthetics and permanent press are especially susceptible to grease stains. Don't toss these into the laundry hamper without pretreatment.

Nongreasy Stains: Soak in plain cool water, overnight if necessary. If the stain is still there, try laundry detergent and a cool water rinse. Be especially careful to avoid using heat on nongreasy or combination stains. There is a high risk that heat of any kind will turn them permanent.

Combination or Mystery Stains: A combination stain is comprised of both greasy and nongreasy elements. Ice cream, gravy, coffee with cream, a cream sauce, or soup are a few examples. Avoid heat! Follow the procedure for nongreasy stains given above. Rinse well and let the fabric dry. If discoloration remains, apply dry-cleaning fluid as described under greasy stains.

Ball-point pen ink does not come off unless special measures are taken. Try dabbing at the ink with rubbing alcohol; then rub with Vaseline. Don't let Vaseline remain on the fabric, especially on synthetics or permanent press; wash it out immediately with hot water and detergent.

If a stain does not respond to first treatment and you decide to forgo dry-cleaning, it can sometimes be removed with Fels Naptha (an old-fashioned yellow bar soap). On bleachproof fabrics, try a mixture of liquid laundry detergent and a few drops of chlorine bleach. Wet the fabric and work in the soap or detergent-bleach solution with your fingers. Then gently rub the stained area against another part of the fabric. Rinse. A grandmother's trick for delicate fabrics: Rub dishwashing detergent into the spot, place the garment into a basin of water, let it sit in the sun, stain side up, for a day to two. The sun is a bleaching agent.

Warning note: Pale-colored, sugar-based stains (ginger ale, grapefruit juice, beer, white wine, and so forth) often dry without any obvious trace. The article is considered clean and put away. As time passes, the sugar is acted upon by yeast, which causes a permanent yellow discoloration. Or the article is cleaned or laundered and heat brings out a stain. Spot-check clothing carefully after you take it off, especially after a party. There's usually a faint mark that indicates where the spill occurred. This is almost always removed by a plain cool water rinse, making it safe to launder the garment normally. Be sure to call such stains to the attention of the dry cleaner.

To avoid food stains on babies' and toddlers' clothing, presoak in cool water. (An overnight soaking is best.) Wash in hot water. A few stains may result but the sanitary benefits of using hot water offset the risk.

How to Clean Everything by Alma Chestnut Moore offers easily understood tips for removing a wide variety of stains, including an assortment of last-ditch methods when all else has failed.

Hand Washing

No special technique is required for hand washing everyday things. Add detergent to water and make sure it is completely dissolved before immersing the clothing. For easier going, prespot and let things soak in water and detergent for at least 15 minutes. The detergent will release most of the dirt, allowing you to swish instead of scrub. A nylon brush, used gently with a bit of extra detergent, handles resistant soil, but don't use a brush on delicate fabrics. Rinse until the water is clean. This means at least two changes of water. If you have too many suds, a small handful of salt in the first rinse will help to eliminate them. Those who do most of their laundry by hand will be happiest with a low-sudsing detergent.

Delicate fabrics, stretch-prone knits, and wool are another matter. These require care and a gentle washing agent. All-purpose laundry detergent is ill-advised, especially on wool. (Many wools are not washable. Check the fabric label.) Liquid dishwashing detergent does a perfectly fine job.

For safest hand washing:

Do one article at a time.

Button or zip knits before washing to help preserve their shape.

Work in cool water. One capful of detergent is usually enough for the bathroom basin. Use a little extra to prespot; let things soak for a few minutes.

Squeeze. Never rub, twist, or wring.

Rinse thoroughly.

Roll in a terry towel to absorb excess water.

Dry knits by spreading flat on top of a terry towel with a few layers of newspaper underneath. Shape by hand to approximate the original outline.

Handle wet wool as little as possible to avoid stretching, shrinking, or matting. Be careful with your iron. Use cool steam or a pressing cloth. Never put a hot, dry iron directly onto wool.

THE FINISHING TOUCH: IRONING

The absolute bottom line of ironing is that one should do as little of it as possible. Life is just too short. There are certain things that need never be ironed including bedding, underwear, towels, jeans, T-shirts, children's everyday things, anything that comes out of the wash looking almost as good as it looks after it's ironed. For acceptable results, however, you are going to have to take a little care in the washing-drying process. Follow the guidelines given earlier and learn to press things into shape with your fingers as you take them from the drier.

Have the right tools for the job. An ironing board can easily last a lifetime, and since the very best deluxe model doesn't cost much more than the cheapest, get the best. Its height should adjust easily so that you can work standing up or sitting down and share it with folks who are larger or smaller than you. It should be light enough to be easily portable but not so light that it tips over easily. Invest in a well-padded fire-retardant ironing board cover and a hot plate for the iron.

An iron only seems to last 10 years or so, but you should still spring for the best. Do not get a very heavy iron. You don't need it with modern fabrics. Do make sure that it is heavy enough to balance securely on the board and get one with a good range of temperature settings. Steam is essential; an additional built-in spray device is hugely helpful in erasing ironing mistakes and stubborn creases.

Care of an iron: Even the best of us slips up occasionally and burns something that melts and sticks to the iron causing it to drag rather than glide. The good news is that the iron can almost always be cleaned. First, try putting your iron on its hottest setting and ironing over a damp rough towel. If that doesn't work, *unplug the iron,* let it cool enough so that it will not burn you and tackle it gently with steel wool (preferably soapless). If you have an iron with a nonstick surface, read the manufacturer's instructions for cleaning, and *do not use steel wool.*

If you are not getting adequate steam, then your steam vents are, no doubt, clogged with nasty mineral deposits from your water. Unplug. Use a paper clip or pin to loosen any solid buildup caught in the holes at the bottom of the iron. Make a solution of one-half white vinegar and one-half water and pour into the steam iron. Replug the iron and turn on the steam. By the time it all steams out, your iron's arteries should be clean and functioning.

Setting up: Ironing is definitely assembly work. Establish your own system to make the job go quicker and cut down on error. *Here are some guidelines:*

Find a pleasant place to work and make sure that it is not in an activity corner.

If you are right-handed, you will be working from right to left. Establish a place within easy arm's reach at the right side of your ironing board to pile your unironed articles. A large basket or wheeled shopping cart makes a good repository.

Have enough hangers and a place to hang finished garments close by the ironing board, and provide a clean, dry surface for folded articles.

Make sure that the floor around you is clean. It is better to clean a floor with a broom than with the sleeve of a shirt.

The square end of the board should be closest to the plug. This should be on your right side when you are facing the board; it will hold the iron when it is at rest. Have your cord plug in an outlet near the right side of the board with a clean run from the outlet so that it will not accidentally get pulled down. If your cord is stretched too tight between board and outlet, it will cut down on your maneuverability. If you use an extension cord, be certain that it is one designed for heavy duty.

If you do not have a spray attachment on

your iron, invest in a plant sprayer to dampen problem areas, and have a lint remover handy.

Ironing can be done while sitting down, although I seem to need the freedom of movement that comes when I am on my feet.

Begin by establishing a piece sequence. Work with a progressively higher heat setting, ironing the articles that require the least heat first. The psychology of drudge work also comes into play here. You are more likely to get everything done in one session if you save the least complex (and easiest) pieces for last. Be sure to allow your iron to cool down adequately if you find yourself going backwards on the heat scale.

Technique: Do not press down when you iron. It is not necessary. Simply guide the iron and let it do the heavy work. For large pieces, iron from right to left with straight, even strokes. Never use two strokes when one will do. Use your free hand to secure the piece on the board. When doing small, fussy things like ruffles or shirt cuffs, stretch the fabric with the fingers of your left hand, work the point of the iron in small deft strokes so you don't crease what you've already done. An iron is a true form-follows-function tool. Manipulating it correctly comes almost naturally because it's so well designed to do the job.

Keep the iron moving. If it stays on one spot, or gets too hot, it can discolor, scorch, or melt your fabric. During long ironing sessions, occasionally turn the dial to a lower setting. The materials used in an iron sometimes hold heat that can build up past the point indicated on the heat control dial.

Use the correct temperature setting for the fabric being ironed (see Fabric Ironing Guide). Your iron is marked with general instructions and often a garment label will indicate more precise settings. If there is any question, or if the piece is not ironing as well as you think it should, then experiment carefully until you are pleased with the results. Do your experiments on a hidden piece of the garment, working your way from cool to hotter settings.

Move the garment away from your body as you work so you do not have to strain to avoid pressing against it. Do the parts of the garment first that are the least important in the overall appearance of the garment when it is being worn. Take care to avoid mussing those areas of a garment that you have already ironed while you are finishing the piece. Save the showiest part of a garment for last and give it your best shot.

FABRIC IRONING GUIDE

Dry or steam	Temperature setting	Fabric to be ironed	Ironing instructions
Dry	Cool	Acetates	Iron fabric on wrong side to prevent shine. Do not dampen, or water spotting may occur.
Dry	Cool	Acrylics (Acrilan, Creslan, Orlon, Zefran)	Iron fabric blends with setting at lowest temperature of two fabrics. Follow label directions for garment care.
Dry	Permanent press	Metallics	Press on wrong side.
	Permanent press	Patent leather	Use brown paper as a pressing cloth. Press on wrong side.
Dry	Permanent press	Suede leather	Cover ironing board with brown paper to prevent suede from rubbing off. Press on wrong side.
Dry	Permanent press	Silk	Iron on wrong side. (Some silk can be steam ironed; consult label on garment.)

Dry or steam	Temperature setting	Fabric to be ironed	Ironing instructions
Dry	Permanent press	Permanent press touchups	Dry iron lightweight durable press 100-percent synthetics. If necessary, remove remaining wrinkles with steam. Use press cloth to avoid shine.
Dry	Permanent press	Polyesters (Dacron, Fortrel, Kodel)	Polyester fabrics launder and dry quickly. A light touch-up may be desirable for resetting pleats, etc.
Steam and spray or dry	Permanent press	Permanent press blends of cotton and polyesters	To help restore creases or pleats, test inconspicuous area. If shine or color changes occurs, use press cloth. Iron dry or with steam and permanent press spray.
Steam or spray	Permanent press	Wash-and-wear cotton, rayons, nylons, triacetates (Arnel)	Steam and/or spray.

197

Dry or steam	Temperature setting	Fabric to be ironed	Ironing instructions
Steam	Wool	Woolens	Steam press on wrong side. Use thin, dry pressing cloth to prevent shine on hard-finished worsted or when using a dry iron.
Damp or steam and spray	Cotton	Cottons, starched clothes, sheer linen	Iron dark colors on wrong side to prevent shine. Iron embroidery and lacquered prints on wrong side to prevent damage. Heavy fabrics should be dampened.
Damp or steam and spray	Linen	Linen	Predampen for best results. Iron table linens on right side to bring up sheen, dark linen on wrong side to prevent shine.

On a bad day, remember that lightning will not strike if you only press the part that shows. After all, half an ironed shirt is better than none, especially when that unironed half spends its active life inside a pair of pants.

How to Iron a Shirt (or a Blouse)

Do the yoke first. It is the heaviest part of the shirt and the least likely to wrinkle as you proceed.

Do the sleeves next. Laundries have special sleeve presses that do not leave a crease. You are not a laundry. It is okay to press a crease into the sleeve, but make sure that both creases match. Fold the sleeve in half lengthwise by finding the seam. The top of the sleeve opposite the seam represents your crease point. Lay one side of sleeve on board facing you. Hold underside firm with your hands as you rest the sleeve on the board. Press one side of the sleeve. Lift from board, turn over and repeat process. Do cuff (without crease). Do the other sleeve. The button front of the shirt is next. Then do the back, resisting any aberrant urge to reiron the yoke. Do the buttonhole line and pocket, if there is one. They affect the appearance of the shirt. Gently stretch fabric around buttonhold line and pocket seams with the fingers of left hand while you iron to keep from ironing in pucker marks. The collar is the showiest part of the shirt. Do it last. Begin with the underpart; turn over the finish with the top. If you are touching up a shirt that came through the washing process practically wrinkle-free, iron front, cuffs, and collar only. It is by far easier to hang a shirt than to fold one, although this depends on closet space. Button the top and third from top buttons so the shirt will not lose its line while hanging.

Folding a Shirt or Blouse

Button top and third buttons from top. Turn the shirt over on the board with its back facing you. Fold a lengthwise third of the shirt back toward you. Do it again on the other side. Fold each sleeve back so that it is parallel with the long line of the shirt, cuff buttons facing up. Fold up the bottom third of the shirt. Fold back the top third of the shirt so that the front is facing you. Smooth front of shirt with your hand. Straighten collar. All folding should be loose. Do not pack shirts tightly in a drawer.

Ironing a Dress

Same as a shirt or blouse, just more of it. Skirt first. Concentrate on the focal points of the dress and make sure that they are smoothly done. If you are only touching up, include the skirt's hem. If the dress has a lot of fussy detail or gathers, iron it inside out.

Ironing Pants

If there are pockets, pull them out and press first. Press top of pants next, fitting waistline over board so front and back are separated by board. Iron while rotating pants around board away from body. Before pressing legs, establish the crease. Place both legs together on board, with seams in center of board, top seam facing you. Press the top of the leg facing up. Lift that leg up revealing second leg. Press top of second leg. Lift pants off board and turn them over. Repeat process. Take special care with creases. Fold into thirds or hang on pants hanger. If you use metal hangers, fold a paper grocery bag over metal to prevent hanger marks.

Ironing Children's Clothes

Don't. But if you do, using a sleeve press as an ironing board is easier.

Ironing Aids

Spray starch is probably best left alone. It scorches easily and with modern fabrics is really not necessary. If you use it, follow directions on can and turn heat down a notch. Aerosol products such as Magic

Sizing give fabric a nice finish and make ironing a smoother process.

PROFESSIONAL LAUNDERING AND DRY-CLEANING

When you are under extraordinary pressure, a week (or month) of outside laundry or cleaning service, expensive though it may be, is one way to make your life easier. Even when your schedule is more or less normal, it makes good sense to send out items that require special attention.

Find the best service available. Many dry cleaners – especially those offering one-hour service – are little better than a coin-operated machine. Clothes are not examined for stains and when spots are pointed out, they receive little more than a perfunctory dab with cleaning fluid (which only works on oil-based soil). Inadequate spot removal means permanent stains. What's more, careless dry-cleaning can shrink fabrics and fade colors. On the other hand, an expert cleaner can add attractive years to the life of your clothes. This is equally true of laundries, but good ones are getting nearly impossible to find. If there is no quality laundry in your area, entrust the existing laundry with nothing more precious than sheets or everyday shirts.

And if you care about stains, prespot! Do the rest yourself, or (unless the tag says launder only) send the garment to a dry cleaner. Having something dry-cleaned, even when the cleaner is less than perfect, is usually safer than no-thought, hot-water-only, vat laundering. Always point out stains and explain what caused them. Some laundries and cleaners will look for loose or missing buttons, or falling hems, and do the necessary repairs for an extra charge.

THE SEWING BASKET

Every household requires a small sewing basket that need contain no more than a selection of colored threads and half a dozen needles. Have at least one heavyweight thread and a strong needle for stitching up torn jeans and the like. Avoid cheap kits; the thread is inferior and breaks easily. A needle threader is a great aid, along with a small pair of scissors. My mother's trick: Never have a safety pin in the house. Don't buy them, and throw them out when they find their own way in. That way you *have* to sew. The familiar saying "a stitch in time saves nine" is correct. Catch the problem when it first appears and you have a small chore. Wait too long and you have to resew the whole darn thing. It only takes a minute or two to work a few stitches.

STORAGE

Try not to overload your storage facilities. Crowding means wrinkled, hard-to-get-at things. Items that are used most often should be most accessible. Relegate infrequently used items to the far end of the closet or to hard-to-reach shelves and drawers.

Long-term storage: Always put things away clean. Washing and dry-cleaning kill moth larva. Although moths are much less prevalent than they used to be, largely because of the rapid disappearance of wool carpeting, a favorite home breeding ground, occasionally, moths – and holes in garments and blankets – still do occur. To be on the safe side, pack woolens with cedar chips (purchased at a houseware shop). These smell better than moth balls and will never be mistaken for candy by the baby. Table linens or clothing that is starched before storing will turn yellow in the closet. Garment bags and paper or plastic wraps help to prevent this, and discoloration from airborne soil, as well.

Day-to-day storage: Use a proper hanger for clothing. Wire designs are not meant for

A Most Useful Stitch

The reinforced seam stitch is easily done and resists breaking. To begin, take three stitches at one time, pulling needle and thread all the way through the fabric. Start your next three stitches where the third stitch began. Continue until your repair is made.

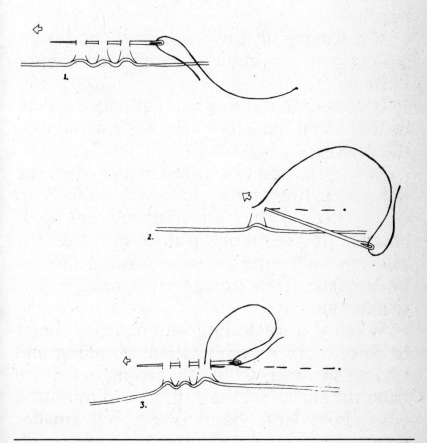

heavy items or long-term use. They leave unwanted creases and offer insufficient support so that things hang out of shape. Use wood or plastic hangers for important items, especially if they spend more time on the hanger than in use. Slippery fabrics cling better to a padded hanger. Pant hangers, which also do pretty well for skirts, help to prevent creases in the wrong place.

Don't hang knits or they will stretch. Fold or roll.

When hanging dresses, shirts, or jackets, zip zippers or close the top and center buttons.

It's easier to roll socks and underwear than to fold them, and they take up less room in the drawer.

Bed linens and towels last longer when use is rotated. Rotation is, however, unlikely to be practiced if they are piled one on top of another. It's too much trouble to lift up the pile to slip the newly washed things underneath. Two storage piles make it easy to alternate.

When you are dealing with matched sheets or towels, try a combination of rolling and folding to avoid pulling the wrong one down from the shelf. Fold top sheets and roll fitted ones. Fold large bath towels, roll smaller ones.

Large households sometimes find that a color key is a useful storage device. When Dick's socks and underwear all have yellow in them and his sheets are green, they stand out nicely from Jane's which are predominantly lavender and blue. Buying a bunch of socks that are the identical color and style is one way of licking the disappearing sock phenomenon. At least the odd socks will match. When tending to group laundry, pile clothing and let everyone put their own things away. Some families spread everything on the dining table *unfolded* in every-man-for-himself fashion.

Eight

Cleaning Like A Pro

My research indicates that there are at least seven ways to clean anything and at least as many exceptions to every rule. Because this is a section and not a book, I have concentrated on all-around methods for easy maintenance of the basic materials found in most homes. If you have more esoteric surfaces to care for, think twice before applying these techniques.

Several specialists have contributed information but the guiding light has been Mary Norton Boyce, a professional cleaner, who is also my sister. Her advice is based on 14 years' experience in which she has done everything from day jobs to heading up the housekeeping staff of a nursing home to running her own small maintenance service. Cleaning is her business. To make it pay, she has perfected speedy, no-nonsense techniques designed to deliver fault-proof, pleasing results.

Safe, effective cleaning demands knowledge of what you are doing. I, for instance, once faithfully waxed a brand new wood floor each month, every month, for a year. My whole decorating plan revolved around its shiny, cared-for appearance. Unfortunately, I used the wrong polish, which completely ruined the finish. I cannot look at the floor today without mentally sanding it back to beautiful. A hired house-hand wrought similar havoc on my kitchen formica by cleaning it weekly with scouring powder. My counter tops are now covered with a network of fine scratches; the eye-pleasing, dirt-resistant sheen is gone forever.

Cleaning is a pragmatic craft. Its skills come with experience. Pay attention to what you're doing and monitor the effects of your efforts. If a recommended technique doesn't give you best results, do some research. Contact furniture manufacturers, read product labels, ask an experienced cleaner, or step into a quality shop and chat with the resident expert. Don't be blindly trusting. Case in point: A friendly neighbor introduced me to the floor wax that wrecked my floor. He was using the same product himself and thought it was splendid. In doing the research for this book, I enquired at a local houseware shop about products for enhancing wood floors. The merchant, in complete good faith, suggested a polish that was essentially the same as the one that had already done so much damage. (To further compound matters, an unclear product label suggested that the polish was safe for use on wood!) Seek counsel from people who really know their business.

Take no chances with your precious possessions. Antiques, in particular, often require special care. Seek out expert advice. Antique dealers are knowledgeable in the care of fine furniture and, when the shop is empty, are almost always delighted to share their knowledge. Museum staff consider it part of their job to answer serious questions.

TOOL GUIDE

The right tools, correctly used, are the hallmark of the professional. Good ones are most effective and almost always easier to use. Don't be satisfied with inadequate equipment. Well-made tools have a long life and in the long run are the best investment.

The best tool *may* be the most expensive, but more often it is from the middle of the line. It's rarely the least expensive. Be prepared to comparison shop. This can be as simple as picking up and trying out the three varieties of broom stocked by your local hardware store instead of blithely choosing one that matches your color scheme. In the case of expensive items, such as a vacuum cleaner, it may mean going from store to store to examine what's available, or arranging for a home demonstration. Whenever you buy, avoid features you don't need. The more complex the device, the more likely it is to break down.

The supermarket is not the right place to find a quality tool, but a houseware or hardware store often has a fair selection. Large, family-oriented department stores are good sources, especially for electrical appliances. Janitorial supply houses are excellent for heavy-duty items such as brooms and mops. With the exception of vacuum cleaners, professional equipment is often a far better buy than standard household equipment; it may cost more but it lasts far longer and is carefully designed to give efficient results. The staff at janitorial supply houses are usually quite helpful. Because most of their business is done by telephone or mail, they have time to talk and rarely ask if you're a pro. While you're there, investigate cleaning products as well. You'll get the largest economy size you ever saw, but the price will be right, and the quality good.

Vacuum Cleaner

Don't try to get along without a vacuum. If you live with few carpets, any moderately priced canister with strong suction will do. If you have wall-to-wall carpeting or sizable rugs, you need a more expensive machine that provides beating or brushing action as well as suction. Gritty particles of dirt and oily airborne soils sink into a carpet where they cling. They are not removed by suction but accumulate unseen and are ground into the fibers and the carpet's base. Eventually, they wear away the fabric, but long before that the floor covering will not come clean despite your best efforts.

The upright vacuum is the tool of professional cleaning people who maintain offices and other places that feature lots of wall-to-wall carpeting. It is a relatively effortless machine that does its job with only a gentle directional push and a firm hand grip. The cleaning head is equipped with a rotary brush that gets deep into pile to lift out embedded dirt. The upright is the best vacuum for carpet, but that's it. It does not maneuver well at corners, on stair treads, or in narrow spaces and it cannot be used to dust walls, windowsills, draperies, carved table legs, or upholstery. Newer models are provided with add-on hose and attachments similar to those of the canister, but in my opinion, the upright is still a cumbersome machine when compared to the jack-of-all-trades canister. It also has less suction power.

The canister vacuum is lightweight and maneuverable, has strong direct suction, and can be used to clean all dry vertical and horizontal surfaces. Suction alone, however, isn't adequate to clean most carpets. More expensive models offer the option of a rug-cleaning attachment with a beating device that loosens deep-down soil. Although this is a major improvement, the canister does not yet match the carpet cleaning performance of an upright.

Of note: Do not purchase either an upright or a canister beating device for Oriental carpet. The pressure can damage the delicate fibers. These flat-piled, tightly woven rugs will get clean enough with an ordinary canister. Shag rugs are particularly difficult to maintain. Consult with a salesperson to get the best possible machine with a shag attachment. The current state of the art indicates that the machine you purchase will be a canister because strongest suction is essential to dig deeply into a dense shag.

There are two types of canisters. One is the traditional tube shape, preferable when you have to vacuum in narrow spaces such as a flight of stairs. The other features a squatter, bulkier body that is less prone to tip and often has space to carry attachments. The mechanical operation of the two types is essentially the same.

Whatever style of machine you purchase, look for one that has a good strong motor and a lot of suction. A retractable, extra-long cord is also helpful, especially because the use of an extension cord is not recommended by vacuum cleaner manufacturers.

When you shop for a vacuum, make sure the demonstration simulates your home conditions. Take along some saved-up floor sweepings and test the cleaning potential of the machine on surfaces similar to your own. Grind in the floor sweepings so they are not just sitting on top of the carpet. Any vacuum can remove surface dust. A good test: Can the machine remove a thread that is clinging to a carpet?

Although in most cases, professional cleaning equipment is recommended, this is not the case for vacuum cleaners. A good standard home model is best for day-to-day needs. Professional uprights are costly, difficult to maintain, and expensive to repair. Industrial wet-dry machines are not especially good at ordinary cleaning functions.

Maintenance: Vacuum cleaners are workhorse wonders designed to give years of service; a broken machine can almost always be easily repaired as long as dust does not find its way to the motor. Some manufacturers will not honor their warranties if you do not use their carefully fitted name brand dust bags. Take this precaution and keep extra on hand. Do not expose your machine to unnecessary risk by using it to suck up large quantities of powdery fly-away substances, such as flour, plaster, dust, and fireplace soot, which can sometimes escape the bag and go right to the motor. Use a broom first to get most of the stuff up; vacuum for final touch-up.

The weak spot of the canister vacuum is the hose, which can clog. Don't vacuum prime offenders like nails; bobby and hair pins; needles and pins; large chunks of pointy, hard debris; and wood slivers. Long vertical objects are likely to get caught crosswise in the hose and nothing you (or anyone else) can do will dislodge them.

When you do not get adequate suction, check the dust bag. An upright's should always be emptied when half full, but sometimes even a canister requires an early change. Small-particled clingy dust can block the bag's pores and make the machine act as if it were full. If emptying the dust bag doesn't solve the problem, remove the hose and place your hand over the suction hole. If suction is adequate at the source, your hose is blocked. Attach the hose to the machine's rear end where the air blows out and be prepared for a dust deluge. If nothing happens, bend a plastic-covered wire hanger and with it probe through the hose, re-applying air and joggling the hose as you do. (Save the hanger when you're done. You will undoubtedly want it again.) If none of these tactics works, you need a new hose.

Storage: Vacuums are stored on the floor because of their weight, although attachments can be hung up. Best storage space is closest to where the vacuum is needed most often. Don't make this tool any harder to get out than you can help and you will use it more often.

Electric Brooms

An electric broom is a relatively inexpensive, lightweight, direct-suction floor cleaner that is the absolutely best supplement to a vacuum for quick, easy pickup of surface dust and crumbs. It is not adequate for regular carpet maintenance but is fine for light touch-up and perfectly OK for floors. Those who maintain a space with small rugs and not much upholstered furniture can substitute an electric broom for a vacuum. When housework is shared, an electric broom plus a vacuum make cleaning chores easier to divide.

When purchasing your machine, look for a long cord, strong suction, and a well-designed dust container that offers the motor good protection and is easy to empty. Don't buy a complicated electric broom with some of the features of a vacuum. Every additional feature adds weight and cuts down on its handiness.

Brooms

With a few exceptions, just about everything a broom can do is better done by a vacuum or electric broom, because no matter how much care is taken, a broom scatters dust. The bristles can also damage carpet fibers and force sharp-edged particles deep into the base of a rug. A broom is at its best as an emergency tool for sweeping up broken glass and heavy substances, such as sugar. As a primary tool, it's most useful in the kitchen where crumbs and spills are more of a problem than dust.

A flexible-bristled plastic broom is fine for most purposes and especially good for smooth floors; a straw broom is a must for heavy jobs such as cement basements or patios.

A large, janitor-style push broom is the best tool for large, open floor spaces, as they don't scatter dust. Invest in a commercial model with a generous supply of *soft* natural bristles. Those with hard straw bristles are meant to maintain cement or stone surfaces; when wet they can be used as long-handled scrub brushes.

The companion tool to a broom is a dustpan. Get a sturdy plastic model with a hole in the handle so it can be stored hanging up.

Whisk Brooms

Used briskly, but carefully, on upholstered fabric, a whisk broom will get embedded dust up where the vacuum can get to it; it is a useful clothing freshener. I do not find it adequate for pet hair or lint removal but prefer a two-sided, long-handled lint remover that works by friction. When purchasing a whisk broom, look for stiff, flexible natural bristles. Avoid too-sharp bristles that may damage fabric.

Wet Mops

Unless you plan to eat from the floor, almost all floor washing tasks can be accomplished with a mop. Choose a sponge design if you only want one wet mop. Although less than perfect, it is an extremely versatile tool. The sponge mop does a first-rate job of laying down self-polishing floor wax, can be used to wash walls, does a good enough job of floor cleaning, and is indispensable for picking up liquid spills. It is less than perfect for washing floors because the sponge holds a persistent residue of water and can leave tracks. In small areas, this can be compensated for by giving the surface a final once-over with paper towels. A string mop is the better tool for a large floor that demands frequent wet mopping.

When buying a sponge mop, look for a simple, accessible squeeze device with rounded metal edges and an easy-to-replace mop head; make sure that replacements are readily available.

Replace the sponge when it starts to flatten out. Pushed beyond its limits, it will no longer serve as an effective barrier between the hard metal of the mop and your floor or walls. Besides, a worn-out sponge no longer cleans well.

The string mop calls for more effort than a sponge mop, but makes faster work of cleaning in large areas. There are wheeled pails equipped with mechanical wringers that make working with a string mop much easier.

If you want to use a string mop, you might as well be serious about it. The dinky little things sold in the local supermarket are totally inadequate. They wear out too fast, leave parts of themselves on the floor, and do not clean well. The very best are the professional type used by janitors. If you buy one, have an eye for the future and pick up an extra head; a worn-out mop head is useless. Look for a smooth handle and a system that allows for easy removal of the head. Remove the head periodically or the metal parts will oxidize and bind the mop permanently to the handle. Store reasonably clean and dry.

Electric Floor Waxers

To do a good job of applying paste wax to a floor, you need an electric floor waxer, but consumer models sold in department stores are not adequate for this difficult job. A heavyweight professional machine is the unchallenged best tool, but as they are costly and difficult to store these are usually rented. Small home models are only useful for applying liquid solvent-based waxes (see Wood Floors) and buffing paste wax back to a shine between applications. There is no reason to use a machine of any kind when applying water-based waxes.

If you decide to buy, don't get a twin-brush machine, which is a compromise tool meant to shampoo rugs as well as polish floors; it is not particularly good at either job. A rented steam cleaner is far better at shampooing carpets and a single-brush model is best for polishing. Get a single-brush waxer and look for the heaviest machine you can find. The heavier it is, the better your results will be. A wet-dry model can also be used to wash floors.

Cleaning Rags vs. Sponges; Dusting and Polishing Cloths

Many professional cleaning people prefer a rag for wet-cleaning jobs. A rag leaves fewer streaks and gets things cleaner than a sponge with its rough surfaces. However, if you prefer to wash with a sponge, do. Cloths are necessary for polishing and dusting and are far more effective than paper towels for wiping surfaces dry.

Should you start a rag collection, save the right stuff. Old flannel and cotton, terry cloth towels, undershirts, diapers, and soft wools are best. Most synthetics (including sheets) are not absorbent enough; fabrics that shed lint should also be avoided. Remove buttons, hard seams, hooks, and the like, and cut fabric into usable pieces before storing.

Terry cloth dish towels, purchased in quantity at an annual white sale, are tops for cleaning. They are soft, flexible, lint-free (after a few washings), and a good size. (Synthetic terry is perfectly fine.) Cut them in half for wet cleaning; use as is for your dry rag.

Consider a sponge a disposable item and stock up at sales. Two-sided sponges (sponge on one side and plastic abrasive on the other) help to remove clinging soil such as bathtub ring. These are available in supermarkets and can also be found in janitorial supply shops.

Rinse rags and sponges after use and let them dry outside the closet. Wash rags in the washing machine. A sour sponge can be freshened by a brief soak in bleach and water, or toss it into the dishwasher.

Dusting and polishing cloths need to be soft and lint-free. Flannel cloths designed for the purpose can be purchased. For some activities, such as metal polishing, you'll need several rags so that you do not rub dirty polish into the surface. Although cheesecloth is often recommended as a disposable cloth, it is rough enough to cause scratches. "Bags of rags" for polishing jobs are sometimes available from paint and hardware stores.

Do not use your polishing cloth for dusting or vice versa. Used interchangeably, the polisher will become dirty before its time and your dustrag will smear polish over the furniture. Gritty particles held in place by polish can also seriously scratch a finish under the pressure applied to work up a shine. A clean polishing rag is essential.

Wash polishing cloths in warm, soapy water and hang to dry; you risk fire if you throw a rag carrying polish remnants into the clothes drier. Although spontaneous combustion only seems to occur in textbooks, it's a wise precaution to store polish-saturated cloths in a covered glass or metal receptacle. An old cookie tin is a good choice.

Scrubbers

A looped plastic wire pad handles most scrubbing jobs. A medium-sized, natural-bristled scrub brush, while not wanted too often, is a good thing to keep in reserve for the occasional floor scrub. Store the brush with the bristles up.

An old toothbrush with some remaining bristle power is great for nooks and crannies. A small, dull-edged butter knife is helpful for getting into crevices and prying sticky matter loose. With a bit of paper towel wrapped around the blade, it is superior to a cotton swab for tiny cleaning jobs.

A toilet brush is an essential. Have one for each toilet and keep it nearby for emergency use. Style is up to you. Whatever does the job and goes with your decorating scheme.

Pails

For heavy cleaning, you should have two pails, one to hold cleaning solution, the other rinse water. Plastic is lighter but metal last longer. A pail should be large enough to hold sufficient liquid when it is half full, as a full pail is an invitation to a spill. Most cleaning formulas call for a gallon of water, so a two-gallon pail is the size to consider. Measuring lines marked on the sides of the pail will help you mix your solutions. Choose one pail slightly smaller than the other so you can store by nesting one inside the other. An indentation in the rim directs the flow of water when you empty the bucket. A small paint bucket is useful for minor sponge jobs. Store wherever you can make the space and try not to keep anything else inside your pails.

Spray Bottles

Spray bottles are convenient applicators that help to control the amount of solution you use and make lighter work of cleaning. Have several so you can premix your regular cleaning agents and have them ready when you need them, those with clearly marked measuring lines are most useful. Small sizes take up less room in the tool carrier. A waterproof marker lets you note the type of cleaning solution on the outside of the bottle.

Garbage Bags and Other Disposable Cleaning Aids

Every cleaning day, I use one large plastic trash bag and pull it behind me as I go to dump all disposable trash and wet and dry garbage into it. This makes big job trash disposal a one-time effort and is a technique used by many pros.

No home should be without paper towels, but for regular cleanup, they are expensive and less efficient than a good reusable cloth rag. If you can't see your way clear to laying in a supply of workhorse rags, investigate reinforced paper "cloths." These are sold in flat, see-through bags and feature a checked design. Every supermarket carries them, and the cheaper imitations are just as good as the name brand. A few used every cleaning day in conjunction with a sponge and two flannel cloths for dusting and polishing will get you through all your washing and wiping tasks.

Conservation note: There are times when disposables are worth every cent and then some. However, this conflicts with our obligations to the home planet. Plastic products, in particular, are environmentally unwise. They are made from petroleum, and don't decay but hang around and clutter up garbage dumps and oceans; when burned, they add unwanted pollution to the air. *But* they can be huge time and work savers! My compromise: When it is almost as easy to use cloth instead of paper, I use cloth. When it is almost as easy to use paper instead of plastic, I use paper. When the use of plastic is unquestionably the easiest way to go, I use plastic *but* as little of it as possible and when practical it's reused.

Squeegees

A squeegee is helpful if you have lots of windows and want to make quick work of washing them. This T-shaped rubber-bladed tool, is used in conjunction with a pail, sponge, and rag, gives excellent, speedy results and saves the work of polishing your windows dry.

Invest in a quality tool with a rubber blade at a hardware store. Measure your windows and purchase a blade as close to exact pane size as possible. If you have small-paned casement windows, the exact size tool will allow you to clean each pane with one stroke. Anything over 12″ wide is too large for easy maneuverability, so large windows call for several strokes. The rag is used to wipe the blade dry between strokes and any absorbent cloth or paper towels will do. Cleaning solution is applied with a sponge and the squeegee never sees the inside of the pail, so your regular bucket is fine.

Do not use a squeegee on cracked window glass. The crack will damage the blade and cause streaky windows. Store so blade is protected from accidental nicks. When windows streak instead of shine, reverse the blade in its holder. When both sides are worn out, replace.

Tool Carriers

It is most efficient to keep small, regularly used tools, rags, and cleaning agents all together in a portable carrying device that can be easily lifted from shelf or hook and taken from room to room. A plastic pail with handle should hold all your regular supplies and leave room for an extra something such as a squeegee or a bottle of furniture polish. Some households, however, require a larger variety of cleaning agents. In these cases, a plastic milk carton makes a good carrier.

For easy transport, screw wheels to the bottom and tie on a pull cord.

Dressing for the Job

Loose and comfortable and lots of pockets. An oversized man's shirt is a marvelous coverall for quick pickups. A small carpenter's apron has convenient pockets.

Hands show signs of abuse faster than any other part of the body so protect them with rubber gloves, which will also block any toxic substances absorbed through the skin. Have two pairs, one for cleaning, the other for dishwashing. But do not wear rubber gloves without first applying a liberal dose of heavy-duty hand cream (not lotion); Vaseline is fine. Without the protective barrier of cream, rubber dries out the skin; with it, you are giving yourself a beauty treatment. Avoid lined gloves. The lining accumulates soil that can kick off a nasty skin condition when worn too long or too often under sweaty conditions.

Rubber-soled shoes or sneakers are a small safeguard against falls and electric shock.

Ladders

Every household needs at least one ladder. Keep a small, light ladder readily accessible and use it for high cleaning. If this ladder is not big enough to get you all the way to the top, make sure that you have access to a taller one when you wash walls or reorganize the highest shelves. Don't try to save time by not using it. A broken leg really slows you down around the house.

Storage

Except for the vacuum cleaner and electric floor waxer, most cleaning tools are best stored hanging up, with those used most often getting choice, easiest-to-reach spots. Hang brooms, mops, and any other handled tools with the working part of the tool off the floor. For easy hanging, drill a hole through the handle and tie a string loop through it. Hang wet mop and rags away from the wall so they can dry with air circulating on all sides. To keep the closet smelling sweet, don't close its door until the mop (or rags) are dry. Pegboard makes a good hanging surface for tools and lets you shift things around without making more nail holes in the wall. Pegboard is available already painted in hard enamel in four-by-eight-foot sheets.

Rather than concentrating all of your cleaning power in one place, consider keeping tools nearest the area where they are most frequently used (the broom in the kitchen, dust rag hidden in the living room, vacuum cleaner in the hall closet nearest the front door, electric broom nearest the dining room, and so on).

The back of the bathroom door is a convenient place to store tools if you're short of space. Cleaning tools are not unattractive and there is no reason why they have to be kept hidden in a closet. The important thing is to store your tools so that they are readily accessible. If you can get to them easily, you will have less resistance to housecare.

SPIT, POLISH, AND...

The prime housekeeping concern is not the simple dirt that comes up with a damp sponge or dustrag but the clinging compounds that adhere to all our surfaces. This formidable soil is the hard fact of cleaning life. It is the result of kitchen activity, airborne auto exhaust, industrial pollution, and human forays into the outside world. Compound soil is not water soluble; a solvent of one kind or another is necessary to get it off. All any cleaning agent does – whether it's plain soap or the most complex secret formula – is to dislodge stubborn grime and help it to float away in the water. The best are the ones that take the least elbow grease and do the least amount of damage to the things you are trying to clean. The same products that handle compound soil also take care of simple dirt and food particles.

Because no two compound soils are alike in their chemical makeup and because the mineral content of water affects product efficiency, no single cleaning agent is all purpose. Those we recommend work most of the time, but you may have to experiment a bit to find products that better meet your needs. If it's easy to use and doesn't damage or build up on the surface you are trying to clean, it's a good product. If it's effective and safe to use on several surfaces, it's a better product. When in doubt, try a direct comparison process, just the way they do it on the TV commercials. Don't make the mistake of using too many different cleaning agents. A small array of well-chosen products that you thoroughly understand will see you through any cleaning day with better and faster results.

Most experienced cleaners eventually come to prefer the simple compounds that grandma kept in her cleaning closet. They are cheap, good at the job, and their strengths and faults are well known. Modern bottled wonders are complex formulas that are constantly being "improved." Just when you think you know exactly what to expect, the formula changes. Besides, using one on most household soil is like using a shotgun to kill a fly; it's more power than you need. With few exceptions, heavily advertised products are expensive and harder than necessary on your surfaces. We suggest some that seem to be bona fide improvements over the old ways. Otherwise, the old standbys are effective at the job and reliable.

The products discussed here are meant for general maintenance of common surfaces. There are others that are helpful in specific situations and these are mentioned where appropriate. (See Household Fabrics; Which Laundry Products; Resilient Floors- Metals; Wood.)

A Shopping List
One or another of these products, used as directed, will handle most cleaning problems. *Keep them on hand.*

Liquid dishwashing detergent: A light-job cleaner that is safe for all washable surfaces. (Do not confuse this with the powdered product meant for electric dishwashers, which is a harsh cleaning chemical.)

Nonsudsing ammonia: An extremely effective solvent for grease and compound soil that is safe for many surfaces; a glass cleaner. Not to be used on leather, marble, soft plastics, varnished surfaces, wallpaper. Can be used on unvarnished wood and household fabrics under certain conditions. Never mix with chlorine bleach or a product that might contain it.

Spic and Span (or a similar product): A big-job cleaner that is effective and relatively gentle and doesn't leave a dull film behind on surfaces. Not for carpeting, leather, marble, soft plastics, upholstery fabric, wall coverings.

Murphy Oil Soap: A big-job cleaner for wood and soft plastics. This can be purchased at a hardware store and some supermarkets.

Liquid chlorine bleach: A stain remover for white enamel sinks and white laminated plastics; a disinfectant for wood counter tops or chopping blocks. Never mix with any other product except laundry or dishwashing detergent.

Baking soda: A deodorizing cleaner recommended for refrigerators; a gentle "scouring" powder that can be used on laminated counter tops and stainless steel sinks.

Lysol Bathroom Cleaner (or a similar product): For bathroom maintenance; safe for fiberglass and colored enamel fixtures.

Bon Ami: For *occasional* use on kitchen and bathroom enamel and porcelain. The gentlest of the scouring powders.

Carbona (or a similar product): A dry-cleaning fluid for stain removal on household fabrics.

Jubilee (or a similar product): This cleaning wax has several uses that are discussed throughout the cleaning section.

Tile 'n Grout Magic: For easy removal of soap deposits, mildew stains from bathroom tiles, shower stalls, grout. This aerosol product (manufactured by Magic American Chemical Corporation in Cleveland, Ohio) is available in hardware stores.

Easy-Off (or a similar product): For oven cleaning. Choose a pump bottle instead of an aerosol, to give yourself more control over this potentially dangerous substance.

A Few Basic Cleaning Solutions

No one cleaning mix can be counted on to do everything. Some soils are easier dissolved by one cleaning agent than another, and not all cleaning agents are safe for all surfaces. All three of the following have their place and are advocated throughout the cleaning section. For convenience's sake, mix in advance and keep in spray bottles. Bigger jobs, such as floor washing, call for larger amounts of a cleaning agent, sometimes in stronger solution. We may discuss these with the job in question. Otherwise, check mixing instructions on the labels of your ammonia bottle and Spic and Span package.

Ammonia Mix (4 tablespoons of nonsudsing ammonia to 1 cup of water): This is a light-cleaning formula that can be safely used on bathroom and kitchen surfaces, grouted tile, hard plastics, metals, mirrors and picture glass, painted walls and wood, vinyl and asphalt floors, windows. If your situation seems to call for more, add a few drops of dishwashing liquid to the mix. Rinse as you see fit, though it's not essential on the above-mentioned materials. Windex is a store-bought alternative. If you select another blue "glass" cleaner, read the label; not all of these products are safe for all surfaces.

Gentle Detergent Mix ($\frac{1}{2}$ capful of liquid dishwashing detergent to a cupful of water): A light-cleaning formula that can be used safely on any *washable* surface, such as leather, marble, soft plastic furniture, wall coverings, and wood. It's the gentlest wet-cleaning agent. Rinsing is discretionary, but, because detergent tends to cling, it will be necessary more often than when using ammonia mix.

Heavy-Duty Mix (1 tablespoon of ammonia, $\frac{1}{2}$ tablespoon of Spic and Span,

1 cup of water): A cleaning agent that I find equivalent in function to the all-purpose liquids sold in the supermarket. It is especially effective on complex kitchen soil, and I feel confident using it on most household surfaces, with the exception of leather, marble, soft vinyl, wall coverings, and wood. It is not to be used on carpeting or upholstery fabric. Although this is gentler than the bottled products, and less likely to dull surfaces, it is somewhat drying. Rinse it from any vulnerable surface, such as a vinyl floor. To buy a ready-made formula, read labels until you find an all-purpose ammoniated cleaner that seems most compatible with your needs. Don't believe everything you read. These are not all-purpose but are rough-and-tough cleaning agents meant for complex compound soil. To preserve your surfaces, and to reduce the need to rinse, use Ammonia or Gentle Detergent Mix for simple light cleaning. If you choose a bottled concentrate, dilute it and keep it in a sprayer so you won't be tempted to use it full strength.

Using Cleaning Products Correctly

Every cleaning agent has its own peculiarities. Don't be too quick to experiment. Read labels, follow directions, pay attention to warnings. Where there's reason to doubt, test first on an inconspicuous part of the thing you are about to clean or polish. Unfortunately, labels do not always tell the whole story and a one-time testing may not be adequate. A wallpaper, for instance, might withstand a few applications of a too-harsh solution before its texture or color shows signs of deterioration. it's wise to understand the care requirements of your surfaces so you can anticipate trouble (see Chapter 9).

A Few Common Problems: The color removing properties of chlorine bleach on fabrics are well known, but few realize that bleach also removes color from hard surfaces. Repeated applications will dull the colors of formica, bathroom tile, and tub and sink enamel. Many household products, including scouring powders and tile cleaners, contain bleach. The now-and-then application does little harm, but repeated use will fade colors or whiten the surface layer resulting in an unattractive grayish "bloom."

Almost all cleaning agents are potentially damaging in strong concentrations. Ammonia, for instance, one of the gentler substances when diluted, can bleach colors if used full strength. All concentrates are very drying, which can cause vulnerable surfaces,

237

like soft plastic upholstery or enamel paint, to crack. Don't use strong products unless they're actually necessary. Rinse thoroughly when you do.

Some products are much stronger than others, and must always be used with the greatest of care. Toilet bowl cleaners, for instance, can etch a permanent ring into the porcelain if you let them sit overlong in the bowl. Never use such a product to remove stains from anything except a toilet bowl. Its potent chemicals can cause adverse effects.

The same is true for lye-based oven cleaners. These are useful in their place, but that place is the oven. Don't use an oven cleaner on any other part of the stove. Drain cleaners should not be used automatically, especially not on a monthly basis as a preventive measure; they are rarely necessary (see page 140).

All scouring powders contain damaging abrasives. After a few years of regular application, they engrave sink and bathtub enamel with a fine network of visible scratches; in 20 years the enamel is worn through. Softer surfaces don't stand a chance. Marble, fiberglass, and plastics should never be subjected to scouring powder. Neither should stainless steel or chrome.

Use gentler products (baking soda, Lysol Bathroom Cleaner, Soft Scrub) for bathroom and kitchen maintenance. Use scouring powder as a regular cleanser only on enamel sinks and tubs that are already so badly scratched that nothing else will get them clean. On intact surfaces, the occasional use of scouring powder on an especially grubby sink or tub is OK, but avoid repeat applications and choose Bon Ami, the least abrasive of the scouring powders.

Despite its abrasive qualities, scouring powder has its value. It's an extremely effective hard surface stain remover that works by taking up a bit of the surface along with the stain. Pros use it (with discretion) to remove *small* stubborn spots from flat-painted walls, floors, and counter tops. Dampen first to make a paste and don't attempt this on a large surface where the negative effects will be too obvious. Scouring powder can also be used to remove mineral deposits from the toilet bowl if not applied too often.

Avoid the overuse of polishes and waxes. These products (discussed in detail throughout the cleaning section) can save work and protect and enhance surfaces, but, used too often, they accumulate in an unattractive fashion and must be painstakingly removed. The trick is moderation. Three times a year is often enough to apply any polishing agent; most home surfaces don't need polish or wax at all. Don't be misled by product-serving advertisements that suggest that a wax or polish should be used every time. Wax-and-clean products are especially prone to build up on surfaces.

When you do wax, use the right product. Oil-based furniture polishes (such as Liquid Gold) and wax-based polishes (such as Jubilee) cannot be applied interchangeably. When one is put on top of the other, the result is a gummy, hard-to-clean mess. Water-based self-polishing floor waxes (such as Future) are for resilient floors, not wood. Liquid solvent waxes (such as Preen) are used most often on wood, not resilient floors although they can be used on any floor except asphalt. (See Polishing; Marble; Metals; Painted Surfaces; Resilient Floors; Wood.)

Detergent buildup is a small nuisance that nevertheless should be understood. Most cleaning agents do not rinse off completely but accumulate on surfaces and eventually become visible. This residue most often appears as a dulling film, but it can look like dirt. Ammonia and Spic and Span (the bases for the cleaning mixes that we recommend) are least prone to build up. Ammonia is a gaseous substance suspended in water that evaporates once it is let out of the bottle. Spic and Span is loaded with water softeners that make rinsing easier. Soaps, detergents, and bottled all-purpose cleaners are the major culprits. A rinse made from a pint of white vinegar and a gallon of water will remove product buildup from hard surfaces (such as walls, glass, and resilient floors). When it happens on carpeting or upholstery fabric as a result of using a rub-in shampoo, try using a steam extraction machine to remove it, or call in a professional cleaner.

The Chemicals in Your Cleaning Life

Every year, thousands of people receive emergency hospital treatment for injuries caused by household cleaning products. Children under five are the most frequent victims. Cleaning chemicals are not benign. The only safe products in the cleaning basket are plain soap and baking soda. The rest are potentially dangerous to health. They can, in fact, be deadly.

Assume that all household cleaners are potential killers and act accordingly. Read product labels and heed warnings. Don't limit your concern to lethal doses. You are exposed to enough pollutants in your normal life, without adding more. Small amounts of some chemicals can accumulate in the body or add insult to existing injury.

There is no effective antidote for several commonly used substances found in furniture polish, oven and drain cleaners, and pesticides. Keep these (and all other cleaning products including laundry detergent) safely out of reach. Do not store a pesticide or cleaning product in a food container and rinse work surfaces well after using one in a food preparation area. If you transfer a product from its own container to a spray bottle or small storage jar, mark the contents on the new container with a waterproof marker. In case of accident, you must be able to name the product so that treatment can be prescribed. Keep the phone number of your poison control center near the phone.

According to the Center for Science in the Public Interest's *Household Pollutants Guide,* "More chemicals are found in the average home than in chemical laboratories of a century ago. Many homemakers know little about these chemicals and even less about their toxic effects when mixed or misused. Labels contain only partial listings of ingredients which are often unpronounceable and mysterious.... No conscientious chemist would handle chemicals such as pesticides and oven cleaners without laboratory hood and rubber gloves, nor disperse aerosolized caustic chemicals through the laboratory. What professionals won't do through an acquired respect for the danger of most chemicals, the manufacturers of household chemicals instruct the average homemaker to do 'with care' using their products."

Never mix products together unless you know it's safe to do so. In one combination or another, bleach, ammonia, and certain acids – common ingredients in numerous household products – produce highly toxic gases that can knock you out before you escape the room. Don't mix bleach with ammonia; don't mix bleach with any product except laundry or liquid dishwashing detergent; don't mix ammonia with any other product unless you are positive there will be no adverse effects. Do not mix any complex product (such as all-purpose cleaner, drain cleaner, toilet bowl cleaner, rust remover, and tile cleaner) with another complex product. Don't even mix one toilet bowl cleaner with another toilet bowl cleaner. Two different products designed to clean the same surface may not have compatible formulas.

Chemicals are absorbed through the skin. Chemical-laden vapors enter through the

243

nose and mouth. Many products dry the skin and, in strong concentrations, can cause burns or set off a painful lingering skin inflammation. A misdirected spray of oven cleaner or a splash of drain cleaner can blind you. Read product labels. If there are serious warnings printed in bold, clear type, know that you have a potentially dangerous product in your hands. Let your skin and nose be your guides as well. If it smells bad or stings, take a few sensible precautions. Open the windows and/or wear rubber gloves. Don't be fooled by perfumes. Lemon-scented lye is still lye. Hold your breath for small aerosal jobs, don't inhale any product that smells like shoe polish or paint thinner, and wear body-covering clothing when you do heavy cleaning. When doing big jobs with powerful aromatic, powdery, or caustic chemicals, take extra precautions. Wear protective goggles and a mask designed to block toxic fumes and minute powdery substances. These can be purchased in any hardware that caters to professional house painters, carpenters, or artisans.

When possible, choose less dangerous alternatives. Corrosive toilet bowl cleaners (a deadly poison and bad for plumbing besides) are almost never needed. When a few seconds with a toilet brush and a little scouring powder will remove most stains, why chance a horrible accident? (In-bowl cleaners are not so toxic, but they're really not necessary.) Squirt bottles, which are more easily controlled by the user, are almost as convenient as aerosols. Use them when they are available to reduce the risk of inhaling a toxic chemical. If enough consumers pick safer alternatives, more of them will come on the market. Manufacturers aren't stupid.

When all is said and done, there is no more reason not to use potentially dangerous cleaning products than there is not to drive a car, take an airplane, or use electricity. Life, after all, is not risk-free. But use them as an informed, sensible adult, and educate others in your home environment.

A PLANNED APPROACH

Most surfaces, in most homes, can withstand considerable neglect. However, there are a few that may be permanently damaged by soil; these should be attended to even when time is tight.

The most vulnerable home surfaces are floors, floor coverings, and upholstered furniture. Plan to vacuum these thoroughly once a week. Sweep or lightly vacuum heavy traffic areas and around the dining table at least once between heavy vacuums. At the same time, vacuum or use a whisk broom on couch and chair cushions, arm and head rests. Sweep the kitchen floor at night after dishes are washed. Wipe up spills as they occur. When you can't fit all this in, pay attention to walkways and favorite seats.

Keep marble, acrylic, and varnished tabletops well dusted; they scratch easily.

If fingerprints and smudges are a concern, spot clean flat painted walls and washable wallpaper regularly.

Surfaces where food is prepared should be kept in sanitary condition.

Don't let laundry pile up for longer than a week.

You can remain flexible about the rest. However, those who manage to stick to a regular cleaning schedule have more comfortable homes and in the long run, do considerably less housework. Try doing a little pickup and cleaning every night so the house is maintained at a comfortable level. No-attention, slow-cooking meals virtually prepare themselves while the work is being done. *Or* assign one night a week to housecare and serve a no-cook meal on paper plates. *Or* do your serious cleaning every other week (once a month, if you can get away with it), but schedule one substantial weekly pickup that includes a heavy vacuuming and thorough dusting. Fit laundry in on the weekend or another evening. With all of these approaches, plan an occasional full cleaning day for chores that can't be accomplished piecemeal.

When to Do What

The following guidelines cover the major chores that keep a home up to snuff. A double asterisk ** indicates an essential job that is best done promptly. A single asterisk * signifies that delay will not cause any great falling off of the house standard. Those tasks that are unmarked are the most easily postponed, or even omitted.

WEEKLY
Change beds **
Dust furniture, shelves, and windowsills and anything resting upon them, *without* moving decorative objects *
Vacuum **
Damp clean furniture and spot clean walls, if necessary
Clean kitchen **
Clean bathroom *
Damp mop floors **
Do laundry **

MONTHLY
(These jobs are easiest done on a rotating basis.)
Shake out or vacuum draperies *
Dust lampshades and light fixtures
Vacuum Venetian blinds
Dust small objects and surfaces beneath them
Examine for cobwebs *
Vacuum under heavy furniture
Fold back area rugs and vacuum under them
Wet mop nonwood floors, if necessary *

AS NEEDED (but usually no more than three or four times a year)
Clean range hood, stove, and oven **
Defrost refrigerator **
Wash windows *
Apply paste wax to wood floors *
Launder curtains *
Clean shower stalls and tiles
Apply polish to furniture

ANNUALLY
Send rugs and draperies to be cleaned, or do them yourself **
Wash upholstery fabric **
Wash walls
Spruce up storage systems *

Cleaning Sequence

To assure that subsequent cleaning actions don't undo those you've already accomplished, tackle jobs in the following order. (Of course, not all jobs are done every time.)

1. A general pickup comes first. Put things back where they belong. Close drawers, closet, and cupboard doors. Collect trash and empty wastebaskets. Open windows to freshen the room.

2. Next come dust-raising activities. Shake out curtains, whisk upholstered furniture, take down drapes, plump up cushions, make beds, change air conditioning filters, and so forth. If you plan to sweep instead of vacuum, sweep now, so that any dust that settles on furniture will be removed with the dust cloth.

3. Vacuum or dust furniture, along with things like molding, picture frames, radiators, and windowsills. Work from high to low, that is, do the top of the table before its legs, the windowsill before the radiator.

4. Vacuum floors and carpets.

5. Damp clean or wash hard surfaces such as furniture, walls, counter tops, and accessories, including mirrors and picture

glass. Spot clean walls. Do damp cleaning before wet.

6. Polish furniture. (To save steps, many cleaners treat dusting, damp cleaning, and polishing as one action. Divide a room into rough quadrants and attend to one area before moving on to the next; follow the dust, damp clean, and polish sequence within each area.)

7. Wash windows, walls, woodwork, etc.

8. Damp clean or wash floors.

9. Wax floors.

SAVING TIME

Any top professional can thoroughly surface clean a typical three-bedroom, two-bath house *in less than four hours*, provided the space is picked up in advance. With practice, you can do this too.

Decide what you intend to accomplish – and in what order the work will be done – before you begin, then stick to the plan. Amateur cleaners tend to do a bit more here and there as they go along and to drift back and forth from job to job. This slows you down and can prevent the day's goals from being met.

Assemble supplies and make sure you have everything you need. It's faster going if you keep small tools and supplies in a portable carrier that moves along with you as you work. If you plan to wash a large area, premix the cleaning agent in a bucket but put if safely to one side to avoid overturning.

Start with an easy job and don't schedule a difficult task for the end when you are likely to be less efficient. Peak efficiency usually comes somewhere in the first half of the cleaning period. Rotate room order from week to week. If you always do the living room first and finish with the bedroom, the living room is probably a bit cleaner than need be while the bedroom consistently gets short shrift.

When two people are involved in housework, work in separate areas for a clear traffic pattern; decide in advance what jobs each of you will do. Pros usually assign kitchen, bathroom, and floor washing to one partner and vacuuming, dusting, damp cleaning, and polishing to the other.

Work to a predetermined deadline. Begin promptly and set a time when you will finish. As further motivation, schedule the end of the workday to coincide with a personal reward that begins at a definite hour such as a favorite TV show or the arrival of a friend for drinks.

Work at a steady pace. Schedule one or

two short breaks to occur after major cycles are completed; for example, eat lunch only after the laundry's done and bed's made. A portable kitchen timer, set to go off halfway through any work cycle will alert you if you're dawdling.

When you become proficient at a given task, work to build up speed. Set the timer to go off 5 or 10 minutes sooner than it took to do the job the week before. When you're comfortable with the new pace, try to shorten the time again. But work only as fast as you can without making mistakes.

The right background music can lift your spirits and help you to build speed and momentum; the wrong ones can do just the reverse. Find your own best rhythms. I am partial to Russian Gypsy music. My sister swears by disco.

If you find that you're overtired or distracted (or are making mistakes), slow down. Sometimes a glass of orange juice and a short, unscheduled break help. If not, call it quits.

Don't hurry through any task you actually like doing. While few of us would claim to enjoy housework, many people have special jobs they find pleasurable. If polishing the silver gives you a chance to recollect or daydream, relax and enjoy it. Plan to save a "favorite" task for the end of the work cycle!

Body Movements
For best cleaning results, take advantage of the superior strength and dexterity of your primary arm. Use it whenever you can, even though many simple cleaning movements can be made with either arm.

When it's convenient, work in the direction of your primary arm. If you're right-handed, dust or polish from left to right. To clean a room, start at the door and circle your way around the room, bearing right. Keep supplies on your opposite side to avoid mishaps. (For obvious reasons, never place them behind you.)

An arm that is slightly flexed has far more control and mobile strength than one that is fully outstretched. Don't stretch too far for any cleaning action but define your working area by a comfortable arm span. (For most of us, this is about three feet.) Your work area can be extended if you use a long-handled tool, such as a mop or hosed vacuum, but you will still achieve better results with your elbow bent.

Large areas, such as a floor or wall, are done in a piecemeal fashion. Concentrate only on an area that you can comfortably reach, then move on to the adjacent area, overlapping slightly to avoid a seam effect.

Bend your knees before lifting a heavy object, even if it's at waist level. Squat when working low, rather than bending over. Bent knees relieve strain on stomach and back muscles.

BASIC SKILLS

Some preparatory pointers;

° Understand the nature of the surfaces you are cleaning and learn their requirements so far as technique and cleaning agents are concerned. Specific care guidelines begin on page 264. Cleaning products – and their pitfalls – are discussed earlier in this chapter; formulas for Ammonia Mix, Gentle Detergent Mix, and heavy-Duty Mix are found on page 234.

° Don't compound cleaning problems. Dust before washing; wash and rinse before waxing; allow surfaces to dry thoroughly before applying wax or polish. Dry-buffing with a clean, soft cloth will often restore a gleam and postpone the need to wax.

° Avoid hard scrubbing. You and your cleaning rag are a powerful duo. Without realizing it, you can rub off paint or scratch a finish. When "it" won't come up, stop before you do damage. Give time a chance. Eventually, the lightened mark may fade or blend back in. The best cleaning touch is a light one, promptly applied.

Dusting
The easiest duster is the small round brush of the vacuum; no special technique is required. To dust by hand, use a soft, clean, lint-free cloth; gather dust toward you and let it fall onto the floor. A light touch is essential to protect the finish of your furniture. Don't flick the dustcloth. Some substances, especially hard plastics, have a strong static attraction to light dust particles. A *slightly* dampened dustcloth reduces the static. Antistatic cloths are also available at a plastic shop or record store. White cotton work gloves (found at hardware stores) make a good duster for carved wood and furniture legs. It's faster going with both hands. Use a feather duster to quick-dust picture frames, barn-sided walls, hard-to-reach shelves, books, and knicknacks. Now it's OK to flick. The feathers hold dust. Most objects maintained with a feather duster need to be dusted with a rag occasionally.

Remove cobwebs from ceilings, high corners and walls with the bare hose of a vacuum cleaner or wrap a cloth around a broom handle; use an upward-outward motion.

Polishing

On many hard surfaces such as wood, chrome or marble, a certain amount of sheen can be achieved simply by rubbing with a soft clean rag (not the dustrag!). Apply a bit a pressure *after* dusting or when you're wiping something dry. When the surface has been waxed, dry buffing will often restore the polished look.

Most polishing is done with a polishing agent, such as silver or furniture polish. This is a cleaning action, since all polishing products – except for those labeled "self-polishing," – contain cleaning solvents to dissolve dirt or abrasives to remove tarnish. Except when using a quick-drying product, such as Pledge, polishing is usually a three-stage operation in which the product is applied, soil is wiped off, and the surface is rubbed to achieve a gleam. For the nicest shine, use plenty of clean rags. A chamois gives a very nice final polish. Apply product to one small area at a time and don't use more than its label directs. Rub polish into the surface; change rags and rub it off again. Use small, circular motions except when polishing silver where straight strokes are advised. Change rags often, as needed. To achieve your final polish, use a fresh soft rag (or chamois) and apply light pressure to a metal surface. With wood, rub harder and follow the grain. (See Metals; Wood.)

Damp Cleaning

The difference between damp cleaning and washing is the amount of water and cleaning agent used. Damp cleaning calls for a minimum of both. Rinse only when the surface is especially sensitive to cleaning agents. Wipe dry if you see track marks or when a sheen is wanted.

In one variation or another, this action is safe for almost all household surfaces, even those that can't take a thorough wetting. Use your own judgment but even careful-as-you-go materials like nonwashable wallpapers and unvarnished wood, can often withstand a *gentle* rub with a *damp* cloth.

Damp cleaning is best done as part of regular maintenance. Keep a spray bottle of Ammonia mix and/or Gentle Detergent Mix in your tool carrier and decide as you proceed when damp cleaning is called for. Keep your eye out for fingerprints and smudges. Give special attention to such areas as tabletops, windowsills, and the walls around light switches. Use Gentle Detergent Mix (or plain water) on wood or any material that calls for special attention; otherwise, Ammonia Mix is preferable.

When a small area such as a spot is involved, dampen a piece of a rag with solution and rub it onto the spot. Gently! To remove an all-over accumulation, spray a little solution directly onto the surface and wipe with a damp rag or mop.

Wet Cleaning

When too much soil has accumulated, when food particles have hardened, or liquid spills have dried, wet cleaning is the only option, *if the surface is washable!* Before applying generous amounts of cleaning solution, be sure the solution is safe for the material and that the material can withstand a heavy application of water. Some materials, notably upholstery fabric and carpet (page 268, leather (page 275), wallpaper (page 290), and wood (page 291) have special requirements. For a choice of cleaning agents see page 231. When large amounts are needed, mix in a bucket and apply solution with rag or sponge. For small areas use a spray bottle.

Remove dry debris and dust before you begin. Then apply solution generously (but not too generously or you will waste time sopping up excess). To avoid dripping on vertical surfaces, wash from the bottom up. Soil will release easier if you allow solution to remain on the surface for a few minutes. With a wrung-out rag or mop, wipe off the solution. Reapply to any remaining spots and use a plastic scrubber if necessary. Wipe with a clean dry rag or paper towel.

To rinse or not to rinse? This depends. If the product's label says rinse, rinse. If you're using a strong concentrate, rinse. If you're about to wax or paint, rinse. The acid test: If the surface looks dull instead of bright and clean, you should have rinsed.

Wet-mopping techniques: To protect walls and baseboards when using a string mop, push a *damp* mop around the outside perimeter of the floor, taking care not to splatter. To do the rest of the floor, use more water or cleaning solution and work backwards. As you move away from the area you are cleaning, mop the floor in front of your feet briskly with a side-to-side swinging action. Old Sailor's trick: To prevent footprints, rest the mop's strings flat on the floor and wipe the bottoms of your shoes across them until your soles are clean.

For a small area such as the bathroom floor a sponge mop is better than a string mop. Use it in a straight back-and-forth, push-pull motion. Sponge mops leave tracks on the floor. Wipe them off with paper towels or your cleaning rag before the floor dries.

To save a double-bucket action, wash the entire floor and then, but only if it seems necessary, rinse.

From time to time, especially in bathroom and kitchen, it's advisable to get down on your hands and knees to deal with hard-to-reach corners.

Sweeping

For effective broom work, you barely lift the bristles from the floor; a too-brisk sweep stirs up dust. Don't swing the broom and don't push up at the end of the stroke. Lift it and use the bristles to pull debris toward your feet; give dust a chance to settle before you lift the broom again. A repeat sweep over the same patch of floor gives most thorough results. A spray of plain water on bristle edges helps to keep dust down. A push broom, which is designed to be pushed, never pulled, is most efficient on large, open floor spaces. (Short, choppy pushes force dirt up from between the cracks of wood floors.)

Sweep accumulations into a pile, then sweep that into a dustpan. In large areas, work in segments and accumulate several small piles. If there's any way to get the last bit of dust into the dustpan, I can't find it. My own technique: Give it two good tries and go on to something else.

Vacuuming

A regular vacuuming regime includes both light and heavy vacuuming. Light vacuuming is a once-over technique, performed frequently in heavy traffic areas, including bare floors; an electric broom is adequate for the task. Heavy vacuuming is harder work, calling for repeat, overlapping strokes on carpeting and upholstery fabric; this becomes dramatically easier when a quality vacuum cleaner is used (see Tool Guide). Households with light-colored wall-to-wall carpeting and young children may find that daily light vacuuming is necessary. For most of us, a heavy vacuuming on cleaning day and a light one in between is sufficient.

With an upright vacuum, the appliance supplies the pressure. Take slow, straight back-and-forth strokes. The controlled speed gives the machine the time it needs for suction.

When working with a canister, apply some pressure to increase suction. Canisters call for brisk back-and-forth, push-pull movements. Don't apply additional pressure when using a special beater attachment, and don't use (or rest) a moving beater attachment on noncarpeted surfaces.

With either style of machine, go back and forth several times over each patch of carpet. Manuals that come with vacuums suggest seven strokes (back, forward, back, forward, back, forward, back). Few of us are willing to do this, although areas such as the piece of carpet in front of your favorite chair might benefit from such attention. Three strokes (back, forward, back) strike me as a rational compromise. Take straight strokes and overlap a bit when moving on to a new area. A quick one-two stroke usually suffices for a bare floor, but adjust the head so that it is as close as possible to the floor's surface.

Professional cleaners vacuum large pieces of upholstered furniture first, following with smaller surfaces, such as windowsills and Venetian blinds. Carpets and floors are done last. Work with the cord behind you. Check to see that the dust bag is not too full before beginning and remove debris from floor and environs so that things like pins, buttons, coins, paper clips, cellophane wrappers, peach pits, and matchbooks are not sucked into the machine.

Get to know your attachments and keep them handy while you work. All hosed systems have a dust brush, upholstery and crevice tool, as well as the floor and/or carpet attachment. The smaller the attachment (and its opening), the greater the suction. The crevice tool has the most suction and is far, far better at pulling out hard to reach dust than the bare hose.

A few pointers: On slat wood floors, adjust the vacuum's head so it lies close to the surface and follow the direction of the boards. When doing area rugs, fold rugs back and vacuum bottom edges and the floor under them. Always vacuum underneath a small rug or doormat placed in a heavy traffic area. Vacuum under low-legged furniture as far as you can reach; very occasionally, get down on hands and knees and reach all the way back or move the furniture. Use a whisk broom (not *too* vigorously) on upholstered furniture before vacuuming in order to release dust so that suction can remove it. Once a month, remove cushions from chairs and couches and vacuum beneath them, using the crevice tool to get down into cracks.

Should carpets show premature signs of wear, your vacuum may be at fault.

Nine

In Alphabetical Order: Care Of Specific Materials In The Home

Ceramic Tile
Glass and Mirrors
Household Fabrics: including Carpeting Rugs, and Upholstery Fabrics; Curtains and Draperies; Slipcovers
Leather
Marble
Metals
Painted Surfaces: including Walls; Woodwork and Furniture; Venetian Blinds
Plastics
Resilient Floors (Asphalt; Vinyl-Asbestos; Vinyl)
Wall Coverings
Wood: including Floors; Furniture; Butcher Block; Paneling

In the following segments, we refer frequently to three cleaning formulas. The directions for making them are repeated here. You might premix these solutions and keep them ready in a spray bottle. For bigger jobs where a bucket is needed, follow product label directions, unless a specific solution is suggested.

Ammonia Mix: 4 tablespoons of nonsudsing ammonia to 1 cup of water.

Gentle Detergent Mix: ½ capful of liquid dishwashing detergent to a cup of water.

Heavy-Duty Mix: 1 tablespoon of ammonia, ½ tablespoon of Spic and Span, 1 cup of water.

CERAMIC TILE

Ceramic tile (glazed or unglazed) should not be cleaned with an abrasive substance such as scouring powder; it scratches! The tile's most vunerable point is the grout that holds it in place. This crumbles under hard scrubbing and is porous, so don't let these surfaces go too long. When you wash, use plain water or Ammonia or Heavy-Duty Mix. Avoid an all-purpose cleaner, which will build up in the grout. For the same reason, don't wax. If you use a scrub brush, don't get carried away. The easiest way to remove stains, mildew, and soap residue from tile floors, as well as walls, is with Tile 'n Grout Magic (see page 234). Clean grout can be protected by the application of a commercial sealer sold in hardware and flooring stores.

GLASS AND MIRRORS

Cleaning glass and mirrors is one of the easiest jobs in the house. Spray on Ammonia Mix (or Windex); wipe clean with a piece of crumpled newspaper; polish dry with a fresh piece of crumpled newspaper. A paper towel or lintless rag can also be used but newsprint actively furthers a shine.

Windows

Small windows are easily done using the glass-and-mirror technique, but larger panes call for a squeegee, the time-saving tool of the professional window washer. Don't attempt the task without a proper tool that has a rubber blade (see Tool Guide).

Mix cleaning solution (3 tablespoons of ammonia *or* 3 tablespoons of liquid dishwashing detergent to a gallon of warm water) in a bucket. Have sponge, squeegee, and a dry rag or paper towels ready. Do one pane at a time. Dip sponge into solution and wring it out so that it's wet but not dripping; use sponge to apply cleaning solution evenly to entire pane; wipe window clean with a squeegee. No polishing necessary!

To use a squeegee:
1. Pull squeegee once along glass from top to bottom.
2. Wipe the blade clean with rag or paper towel; repeat after each stroke.
3. Take another stroke, overlapping slightly with the one that went before.
4. When you've done the entire pane, use a rag or paper towel to sop up moisture that has collected at the bottom of the glass.

To squeegee a large window, work in an "el" pattern:
1. Begin at the upper left corner of the window, if you're right-handed. (Lefties reverse.)
2. Pull squeegee horizontally across the top of the glass until you get to a blade's width of the right corner.
3. Take a right-angle turn and continue down the glass to the bottom.
4. Wipe off blade.
5. Repeat Steps 1–4 in a diminishing "el," overlapping strokes slightly, until you run out of glass.
6. Mop up moisture from the bottom when done.

Don't wash windows on a sunny day. The sun dries the solution too fast, streaking the panes. In very cold weather, a few drops of alcohol added to the cleaning solution will prevent it from freezing on the glass.

HOUSEHOLD FABRICS

Carpets, Rugs, and Upholstery Fabrics

Cleaning carpets and upholstery is a tedious job that requires special equipment. If you have valuable wool carpeting or nonwashable upholstery, call in an expert whether you can afford it or not. Choose your expert with care. A couch of mine was nearly ruined by a cleaning team sent out by one of New York City's most prestigious department stores. Personal recommendation is the best way of tracking down quality craftspeople.

If your carpet or furniture is fairly standard washable modern, you are safe doing the job yourself as long as you follow directions, but do check the cleaning code on upholstery labels to be sure. Use a steam extraction machine. Other methods do not adequately remove the shampoo and are much more likely to overwet the fabric. Rent your machine from a reliable source and use

the shampoo recommended by the manufacturer, as well as a pre-treatment product
for stains and heavy traffic areas. Read
instructions carefully and test products
on a fairly large, inconspicuous patch of
material. Look to see if color is affected
or if material shrinks, mats, or stretches.

Shampooing Carpeting

Move furniture out of the room if you can
when you shampoo carpeting. Otherwise,
protect the carpet by placing thick wads of
aluminum foil or plastic wrap under
furniture legs and protect the furniture by
wrapping foil or plastic around the legs.
Vacuum thoroughly. Pretreat stains and
heavily soiled areas. Shampoo.

The greatest threat to carpet welfare is
stretching, which does not always show up
in spot testing. To avoid trimming and
retacking wall-to-wall carpet, do one three-
by-three-foot area at a time and follow a
checkerboard pattern the first few times it's
shampooed. Work an area, skip an area, work
an area, skip an area. Start at one side of the
room and work your way over to the far side,
maintaining the checkerboard pattern. Then
go back and pick up the patches you've left
out. Continue this procedure until the job

is done. Repeat the action on any areas that still show soil.

Don't wet down any one area more than three times. Remove as much moisture as possible with the suction device. Let the carpet dry for a few hours before walking on it; keeping it clean by walking barefoot until the carpet is dry. When you reinstate furniture, put thick pads of plastic wrap or foil under the legs to keep the carpet from flattening out. Leave the pads for several days. When carpet is totally dry, vacuum. If pile has gone flat, vacuum often for a few days; the pile should perk up.

An outside cleaning establishment will do a far better job on an area rug than anything you or an extraction machine can hope to accomplish. Avoid using a foam carpet shampoo for all-over cleaning. These build up so quickly on the surface that it's a waste of your effort to apply one.

To shampoo upholstery fabric: Use the small wand attachment of the steam extraction machine and follow machine instructions. Take care not to overwet. To protect the filler materials underneath, try to wet fabric only and work quickly. On large pieces, shampoo one section at a time, applying shampoo and sucking up moisture before moving on. Finish the whole piece and examine it. Go back over areas that seem to need a bit more attention.

Should you decide to forgo the machine and use one of the products sold in the supermarket, follow package instructions carefully. Work a small area at a time and blot dry with a clean towel as you go along. These products *all* accumulate on fibers and attract new dirt. When your couch or chair will no longer come clean, try the extraction method or call in a pro.

Warning Note: Not all upholstery can be wet cleaned. Satin, silk, most velvet and velour require dry-cleaning techniques. Follow cleaning code labels. There are methods for home cleaning nonwashable fabrics, but they are not recommended. It's work that is best done by a professional.

Spot Cleaning Washable Upholstery Fabric and Carpeting

Although few cleaning authorities agree, many householders feel that washable upholstery fabrics sometimes benefit from *damp* cleaning on places like armrests. Wring out a cleaning rag in Gentle Detergent Mix to which a few drops of ammonia have been added; gently wipe over the surface without trying to get down deep. To postpone detergent buildup repeat the action with a damp rag that has been well wrung out in water. The same technique may also prove useful on the heavy traffic areas of carpeting. Use your own judgment and in both cases take care not to overwet.

Attend to spills as soon as they occur. Grab a handful of napkins or run for a towel and *blot* up whatever you can. No rubbing. When semi-solids are the problem, use a dull knife to scrape away as much as possible. If the spill is already dry, use the vacuum to remove it. Only after you have gotten off as much as possible should you proceed with stain removal. This is a chancy art that depends on the chemical nature and age of the stain, the fabric to which it is adhering, the unseen pollutants that are already on the fabric and, it seems, the cycles of the moon. For an excellent in-depth discussion, see *Super Economy House-cleaning* by Lois Libien and Margaret Strong. For now, the following – or a variation of it – is the most commonly used technique that works most (but not all) of the time on washable carpeting and upholstery.

Pretreat nongreasy stains (such as urine, blood, alcoholic beverages, fruit juice) with cool water. Use a sponge to dab the water onto the stain, continuing until little or no visible trace remains. Work from the outside of the stain in and avoid rubbing. Don't overwet; blot the surface with a clean white or colorfast rag or with towels whenever the fabric feels too wet to the touch. For all other stains (and to ensure that no trace of a nongreasy stain remains to yellow with time), mix a solution of one capful of dishwashing liquid to two cups of water. Using the dab and blot technique just described, work the stain until you have removed as much of it as you can. This may take quite a while. Follow by dabbing with cool water to remove as much of the detergent as possible. Blot well and speed up drying with an electric fan.

If any discoloration remains after the fabric is dry, try a dry-cleaning fluid (such as Carbona). Saturate a white or colorfast rag (not a paper towel) and dab repeatedly, blotting occasionally. Try to wet only the fabric; furniture filling or carpet backing or padding may be damaged by the solvents in dry-cleaning fluid.

Warning Note: If this method doesn't work, you may find it impossible to remove the stain; anything done to a staining substance is likely to change its chemical composition and render the stain permanent. When it really matters, blot up as much of the stain as possible and get *speedy* professional treatment.

Curtains and Drapes

For nonwashables, a monthly vacuuming with the upholstery attachment will cut down on dry-cleaning bills. Start at the top and work down, and do both sides of the curtains or drapes. On vacuuming days in between, give a gentle shake to dislodge dust.

With washables, vacuuming is discretionary. If you've kept them, follow the laundering guidelines provided by the manufacturer. Otherwise, use an all-purpose laundry detergent and warm water. To prevent wrinkling, bypass the final spin in the washing machine, or hand wash in the bathtub. To wash by hand, presoak for $\frac{1}{2}$ an hour in detergent and water and swish gently. When you use the tub instead of the machine, it's unnecessary to remove drapery hooks, because designs of fairly recent vintage seem to be rustproof. But be careful to avoid pricking your fingers and tearing the fabric. Badly soiled white synthetic sheers and lace curtains respond beautifully to a presoak in $\frac{1}{4}$ cup of automatic dishwasher detergent and $\frac{1}{2}$ tub of hot water. Wear rubber gloves and don't try this on colored curtains as this detergent contains bleach.

Don't wring to dry. Arrange the curtains over the shower rod until they no longer drip. Hang them at the windows to finish drying, spread open so wrinkles can fall out.

Slipcovers

Slipcovers, even those that are proclaimed as washable, seem to look better if they are dry-cleaned. But if you wash them, do it in the machine following the correct procedure for the fabric. Close zippers before washing and avoid hot water; machine dry for a few minutes only. Covers must be replaced on the furniture while still damp so they can dry to fit. Stretch out ruffles and seams with your fingers. Ironing is rarely necessary but if there are wrinkles, steam-iron them out with the covers on the furniture.

LEATHER

Leather is easy to maintain with a bit of special care. Dust regularly. Wash once a month with a damp rag wrung out in light-duty detergent mix; wipe again with a damp rag, wrung out in plainwater; polish dry. Leathers are sometimes darkened by water. If this seems to be the case with yours, inquire at the shop where the piece was purchased to find out what cleaning method is recommended or wash as suggested above and live with a darker color. Some people polish leather furniture just as they polish their shoes. This is not a less-work approach but, when properly done, can result in a beautiful piece of furniture that is somewhat more resistant to soil and stains. Polish also conditions and keeps the leather from drying out. Although some authoritative sources suggest that any *wax*-based furniture polish can be used, and some even recommend lemon oil, I suggest you find a store where fine leather furniture is sold and follow their recomendations.

MARBLE

Marble is a hard-to-maintain substance that is especially susceptible to scratching and staining. For those who are willing to live with less than the best, maintenance is fairly simple. Vacuum or dust often, wash with water and dishwashing detergent and a *few* drops of ammonia, rinse. Polish table and counter tops dry. Avoid scouring powder and abrasives. Mop up liquid spills immediately. Some protection can be gained with paste wax, but eventually this will turn light-colored marble yellow.

Should you own a truly lovely example of this vulnerable stone and wish to keep it at its best, it is necessary to use special products. Quality houseware shops carry stain removal kits, detergents, and waxes created exclusively for marble care. Get them and use them. Vacuum marble floors daily. Dust tabletops lightly with a dry cloth, followed by a wipe with a damp, clean rag. Refrain from serving Bloody Marys or Orange Blossoms without coasters on a marble cocktail table. Acids, even weak ones, etch the surface.

METALS

Brass, Copper, Silver, and Pewter: Buy a polishing cleaner specially formulated for the metal you want to shine and follow its directions, after first washing in sudsy water. (See page 256 for polishing tips.) Spare yourself the work of removing tarnish by storing metal objects in sealed plastic bags, *never* plastic wrap. Always dry metal well after washing it. Do not use "dips" to clean any metal, especially silver or pewter. These products are made from highly corrosive acids that can mar a soft metal's finish.

Some brass and copper pieces are protected by a coat of shellac. Use a metal polish on one of these and you will end up with a scuffed-up mess. Clean with a damp rag and detergent mix; wipe with a damp rag and plain water; dry well with a soft rag; don't rub too hard. Use acetone (purchased at a hardware store) to remove an old coat of shellac.

Of possible interest: The natural discoloration that appears on the surface of decorative metals is considered a form of patina by collectors. It adds monetary value to antiques. Although you may not choose to live with a lifetime of tarnish on your candlesticks, you really needn't polish too often. A bit of softening tarnish on silver, pewter or brass has its own aesthetic attractions if you give yourself a chance to discover them. Besides, most metal cleaners contain abrasives; every time you polish with one, you remove a bit of the metal. Try rubbing the surface with a soft rag dipped into full-strength ammonia; rinse and dry well. This routine will help keep discoloration from building up and give a soft sheen.

Chrome: It is wasted effort to try to keep chrome bathroom and kitchen faucets polished. They are completely undone by the first drop of water. Clean with whatever nonabrasive cleaner you use on the sink or tub. Vinegar will dissolve soap film. Use neither scouring powder nor steel wool. Polish with a dry cloth when there's a special social occasion.

As for chrome kitchen appliances, use whatever cleaning product you normally use on your kitchen surfaces, but not scouring powder or steel wool. Use a plastic scrubber for rough spots. Stubborn soil responds to silver or brass polish. Polish dry with a rag or towel.

If you have chrome furniture, simple dusting and damp cleaning with Ammonia Mix does the job; rub dry with a soft rag for a shine. The appearance of scratched chrome can be improved with a chrome wax purchased at an automobile supply shop.

Stainless steel is cared for in the same manner as chrome. Use dishwashing liquid or baking soda to clean the kitchen sink. Lighter fluid sometimes removes stains. If rubbing it on doesn't work, saturate a piece of cotton with the fluid, place over the stain and cover with plastic, so it won't dry out too fast. The stain may be gone in an hour or two. Scratches can be erased with *very fine* steel wool purchased at a hardware store.

As long as wrought iron doesn't get wet, it's almost indestructible. Dust when necessary. To brighten, squirt Endust directly on the surface; rub it off with a dry rag. If your wrought iron has curlicues, wrap the rag around your finger. Should cleaning with water seem absolutely necessary, use any cleaning agent but work fast and dry the surface *totally* to prevent rusting.

PAINTED SURFACES

The first techniques are preventive. Cut down on finger marks by using doorknobs and light switches, don't lean against walls unnecessarily, or brush against them in passing, protect them from the backs of furniture and be careful when hanging pictures. When washing or waxing a floor, be careful not to smear baseboards.

Maintain by spot cleaning with Ammonia or Heavy-Duty Mix; use a dab of dampened scouring powder or a soft-scrub cleaner on tenacious marks. Occasionally vacuum areas where airborne soil collects conspicuously, such as the wall surrounding the air conditioner, with the dusting attachment. With luck, this may be all that's needed.

Washing an entire wall is hard and messy. Avoid it if you can. Sometimes, scuffed-up woodwork, a badly used hallway or one door in really poor condition creates the impression that every wall needs washing. Take care of these first, and you may discover that the rest can be postponed.

Gloss and semigloss painted surfaces

almost always come clean. Flat paint is problematic; the results may not be worth the effort. Because it is not much more difficult to apply a water-based paint than to wash a wall, wash just a patch before going ahead. If it doesn't look good enough, paint instead.

For normal soil, use a solution of Spic and Span and warm water ($\frac{1}{2}$ cup to a gallon of water). For heavy soil, add a cup of ammonia to the mix. Use a steady ladder when you wash high areas. Work one area at a time, covering only that wall space that is within easy reach. Wash and rinse *or* dry one area before going on to the next. Avoid both rinsing and drying. Every time you go over a painted surface with a rag, some of the paint comes off. Wiping dry is usually adequate; if the wall streaks, use a damp rag that's been well wrung out in clean water. If you're adept, you can wash a wall with a sponge mop. Give it a try.

Professionals wash walls from the bottom up because the cleaning solution may leave permanent tracks as it drips down the wall. This is a more arduous procedure than working from the top down. test first. if the drip marks come off, start at the top.

Don't wash ceilings unless you absolutely have to. Do them before walls and dust first using a towel wrapped around a broom's head. Use a sponge mop.

For easy maintenance, painted doors, woodwork, windowsills, and furniture should be painted with a gloss or semigloss enamel. Wash with a Spic-and-Span solution, boosted with ammonia for heavy soil. Use a plastic scrubber and full-strength ammonia or all-purpose cleaner on scuff marks; rinse. For easier going, maintain these surfaces with a cleaning polish such as Jubilee. These soft-sheen waxes are rich in cleaning solvents and don't build up readily on a surface when used in moderation. Instead of using a water-based cleaning solution, wax a few times a year. In between, damp clean with clear cool water; spot clean with a dab of wax. Buff well after applying polish.

Dust Venetian blinds at least once a month. Lower blinds and pull them to a closed position. With either a damp rag or the small vacuum cleaner brush, wipe horizontally from top to bottom, one slat at a time. Finish one side, pull cord to turn slats over and proceed on the other side. Eventually, despite your best dusting efforts, the blinds will have to be washed. This can be done in the bathtub by two people. Line tub with a sheet or a plastic drop cloth, and fill the tub halfway with warm water, 1 cup of Spic and Span, and $1\frac{1}{4}$ cups of ammonia. Slip closed blinds into the tub and let them soak for 10 or 15 minutes. One person can lift the blinds up and out of the water and hold them against the wall, while the other sponges them off with the solution from the tub. Pull cord to reverse the slats; repeat the sponging action. Slip blinds back into tub, and drain the water from the tub. Lift blinds up against the wall again and repeat the earlier action, this time with a damp rag wrung out in clean water. Let blinds rest in the empty tub until they are no longer dripping wet and then rehang. To speed drying, drop blinds to full length and open slats.

You may find it easier to use a cleaning service (look in the Yellow Pages under Venetian blinds). For an additional charge you can have your blinds restrung at the same time they are cleaned.

Don't wax blinds!

PLASTICS

Surfaces made of acrylic, such as Plexiglas and Lucite, scratch easily. Never clean them with abrasives; avoid heat, hot water, dry-cleaning fluids, nail polish and remover, and alcohol and alcohol-based substances such as perfume. Protect tabletops from scratching.

Dust with a soft, damp rag to reduce static electricity. Clean with Ammonia Mix. Antistatic cleaning solutions, which also are good for perpetually dusty TV screens, are sold at plastic specialty shops.

An automobile paste wax will help to prevent scratches on tabletops and soften the effects of those that already exist.

Plastic laminate is a tough, easily maintained material, but knife and burn marks are permanent and stains are difficult to remove. Protect laminated kitchen surfaces by using cutting boards and protect them from hot pots. Don't rest cans on a wet surface; be careful of spilling substances that stain, such as tea or grape juice.

Any nonabrasive cleaning agent is safe. Stains can often be removed from a white laminate by wiping it down with chlorine bleach. For stubborn stains: Saturate a pad of cotton or a rag with bleach; place over the stain; cover with plastic so it will stay damp; leave overnight. Colored laminates fade when they are bleached. Sometimes a sprinkle of lemon juice or baking soda or a combination of both will remove (or lighten) a stain. A dab of dampened scouring powder is a method of last resort, since it causes scratches and may not remove the stain. Don't make the too common error of using scouring powder for all-over cleaning.

When a plastic laminate loses its gloss, a cleaning wax like Jubilee will perk it up. Wash well with detergent or Spic and Span; rinse and let dry for at least an hour before applying wax.

For vinyl upholstery, Gentle Detergent Mix is less drying than other cleansers. Murphy Oil Soap can be used for heavy soil. Polish purchased at an automobile supply shop will help to restore luster to a dull or faded surface.

Don't use scouring powder on a bathtub or sink that's made of plastic or fiberglass (see page 238).

RESILIENT FLOORS (ASPHALT, VINYL-ASBESTOS, VINYL)

The first rule of maintenance is to forget all those TV commercials where the wax-and-clean hucksters make their pitch. Sweep or vacuum these floors often; damp mop with plain water or Ammonia Mix every week, more often if soil is heavy. Once in a blue moon, but only if they actually look dirty, wash with our Heavy-Duty Mix. That's all.

A no-wax floor will hold its shine for years with this treatment and other resilient surfaces will be clean even though they don't shine. Modern resilient floors are tough surfaces that can easily withstand normal wear without the added protection of wax. Give them a chance to do their stuff. As for the polished look, it seems to me to be a little like face makeup. Some women wear it, others don't.

It's true that water-based waxes are marvelously easy to apply. After washing the floor, you pour one out of a bottle, smear it on with a mop and voilà! a shine. But that shine is made of hard stuff that doesn't come up as part of a normal cleaning operation. Every time you polish, you seal over a remnant of the wax that went before, along with some dirt. Self-polishing floor waxes should be removed at least once a year, even when the floor still looks OK. Those who wax frequently should remove wax after six to eight coats. This is hard work. It is, in fact, the biggest problem in resilient floor maintenance.

If you decide to wax, use Future. This acrylic-based product does not yellow on floors and is somewhat easier to remove than other brands. Today, it is the best self-polishing floor wax in the supermarket.

There may be better brands tomorrow because manufacturers are constantly making improvements. It's perfectly safe to use paste wax on vinyl flooring (not asphalt), but not advised. It's too much work. Don't mistakenly apply a solvent-based liquid that is meant to be used on wood. Those designed for resilient flooring can be identified by a notice on the label stating: "Don't shake" and "Keep from freezing."

A clean sponge mop predampened with plain water, does a perfectly fine job of laying down wax. Rinse sponge well under warm running water then you are through.

Before waxing, mop well using an ammonia solution. Rinse thoroughly with plain water. Between times, clean your floors with a damp mop wrung out well in cool water. *An old wives' trick:* Follow mopping with a cool-water rinse to which you have added a splash of your regular polish. This may prolong the life of your shine.

Polish wears off in heavy traffic areas and stays more or less intact in the places of less use. To avoid irregular buildup, apply polish more frequently to walkways.

The easiest way to remove wax buildup is with an ammoniated stripper purchased at a janitorial supply shop. Follow package directions and open the window; the fumes are likely to blow you away. A mix of $\frac{1}{4}$ cup of Spic and Span, 1 cup of ammonia, and $\frac{1}{2}$ gallon of *cool* water is another alternative, but it's harder going than with a commercial stripper. Avoid using an all-purpose cleaner. More likely than not, it will only soften the wax, not remove it. Whatever solution you use, this is a hands-and-knees job, done piecemeal fashion. Spread solution over as much of the floor as you can comfortably reach. Allow it to stay on the surface for three to five minutes to soften the wax. Then, scrub with a plastic scrubber and lots of muscle. Remove solution (and old polish) with a damp sponge or rag. Repeat until the entire floor is done, changing solution when necessary. Sometimes a second go-round is necessary. To test, rub the edge of a coin across the floor's surface. If it gets gummy, repeat the action. Rinse thoroughly.

The general consensus is that the shiny finish on no-wax floors will eventually wear off. Knowing this, some people, begin waxing immediately to protect their no-wax finish. This is pure folly. Don't wax unless you have to.

A compromise measure, to be applied only after the flooring has lost its shine: Clean well and apply a liquid "floor dressing" sold at a store that sells resilient flooring. Repeat in a year or two.

Another easily avoided problem is detergent buildup. Bottled all-purpose cleaners contain detergents that can leave a dirt-catching residue. This, too, builds up on the surface, to dim the color and fill cracks and engraved designs. To avoid it, use ammonia for light cleaning and a Spic-and-Span mix for serious cleaning. To remove detergent buildup: Wash with Spic and Span, followed with a vinegar rinse made from 1 pint of white vinegar and a gallon of water; finish with clear water.

Sometimes the gleam is lost on no-wax flooring because of detergent buildup, not wear. Test first by *gently* scraping with the edge of a coin, after wetting with cleaning solution. If this reveals the original shiny finish, you are dealing with product buildup, not a worn-out surface. Rent a heavy-duty floor waxer that is safe to use with water. Wash the floor with the machine's scrub brush (not steel wool, unless you want to start a wax regime immediately), and an ammonia and Spic-and-Span solution. Rinse with a mop, one gallon of cold water, and one pint of white vinegar. Rinse again with plain water. Polish with the floor waxer's polishing disk. In the future, avoid the use of bottled cleaners.

WALL COVERINGS

Some wall coverings are washable and some are not. before washing, do a patch test with the cleaner you intend to use. Look to see that the covering does not come loose from the walls, that colors don't fade or run, that the texture doesn't change. If everything checks out, cautiously follow the general guidelines given for painted walls (see page 280), with the following modifications:

For washable wallpapers, dilute washing liquid (3–4 capfuls to a gallon of water) is generally preferable to a stronger solution. Use a damp, not wet, rag and be gentle.

Vinyl and plastic-coated surfaces can withstand stronger cleaning agents and some scrubbing action. Detergent mix can be used, but Spic and Span or ammonia is better for heavy soil.

Nonwashable papers can't be washed. Paint stores sell a dough-like substance that cleans rather like a big eraser. Follow label directions and don't rub too hard.

Ink marks are sometimes loosened by a touch of alcohol-based hairspray. Pencil marks yield to an eraser. There is an aerosol product that removes some stains from wallpaper, but it can leave a ring. A paste made from cleaning fluid and cornstarch will sometimes do the job as well. Dab onto the stain; let dry; brush off. Light rubbing with moistened baking soda may remove a stain with only minimal damage to the surface. Plastic wall coverings can usually withstand a sponge moistened with full-strength all-purpose cleaner to remove scuff and crayon marks; a touch of Soft Scrub may dislodge a small stain.

WOOD

The basic rule for wood care is that water should be used very sparingly and only when absolutely necessary. Water swells, warps, and discolors wood, and lifts its grain. It can also loosen fragile veneers or parquet floors that have been glued down instead of nailed. Wash your wood surfaces as infrequently as possible and only when the protective seal is intact.

Almost all wood furniture and flooring has a "permanent" seal of one kind or another to protect it from wear; all of these can be worn away by use. When this occurs, water should not be applied to a wood surface. To test, put a drop of water on a worn-looking area. If the water beads without being absorbed into the surface, the seal is intact, and water can be used safely *in moderation*. Damp clean wood surfaces only when soil is apparent or after a spill, using a water-dampened mop or rag. When more strength is needed, use a small amount of Gentle Detergent Mix. Although it's not advisable to wet clean wood, sometimes it's necessary. When you must, wash small areas at a time, and rinse and dry as you go. Don't use a heavy-duty cleaner or ammonia. Murphy Oil Soap is good for heavy cleaning. A wood specialist can be of help; discuss your problem with one.

Wood Floors

In my experience, there is only one expedient treatment for wood floors and that is a triple coat of satin-finish polyurethane varnish. It looks great, and it is a tough, durable, damp-moppable finish that doesn't need waxing. With reasonable care it can last for years without having to be refinished. Wax looks great, too, but it is about as durable as a snowflake and there is no easy-to-apply self-polishing wax meant for wood. However, applying wax to a wood floor is not a cosmetic gesture, as it is in the case of resilient flooring. Not only does a wax coat greatly improve wood's appearance, it protects it from scratching and staining and there are solvents in wax that remove dirt and dissolve old wax.

Unfortunately, waxing a wood floor properly is *very* hard work. Paste wax is recommended by floor care specialists; it must be applied three or four times a year, depending upon the amount of wear.

The directions on some water-based, self-polishing waxes suggest they can be used on varnished wood floors, but this type of wax builds up badly and eventually discolors (see Resilient Floors). Inevitably, in the process of removing it, you will damage the finish. Applying such a product to a wood floor is ill-advised. Non-polyurethane satin finishes should be waxed, but the proper product to use is paste wax. Although I would never do it myself, satin-finished polyurethane can also be waxed; again, the wax to use is paste wax. Do not wax a glossy varnished surface. It will not be absorbed into the hard surface.

Painted wood floors are troublesome to maintain. No matter how good the paint, it soon chips and wears off underfoot. A top coat of polyurethane makes it more lasting, but polyurethane has a slightly yellowish cast that affects the color. Paste wax is not absorbed. One protective measure that has been recommended: Apply six thin coats of Future self-polishing wax, an acrylic-based product meant for resilient flooring. For best results, wax immediately after paint has dried and allow each coat of Future to dry thoroughly before applying the next. Maintain this shiny surface with a damp mop wrung out in cool water, at least once a week. Ideally no more than once or twice a year, wash with cool water and light duty detergent mix, rinse and apply a coat of Future.

Do not try to paste wax a floor by hand. You will be exhausted when you're finished and terribly disappointed with the result. Avoid the twin-brush waxers for rent at local hardware stores and supermarkets, which do not clean or buff properly. The only machine that is adequate for the job is a heavy-duty single-disk floor waxer, found where professionals rent their tools. Purchase cleaning disks where you rent your machine and make sure you get enough of these.

Butcher's Wax is a good supermarket product. There are other products available at wood specialty shops, some of which are tinted to match the color of common floor finishes.

How to apply paste wax – preparation and method:

° Vacuum the floor thoroughly.

° Open a window and be careful with matches.

° Wear rubber-soled shoes. Unbuffed wax is slick stuff.

° Practice with the machine until you're comfortable with it. These waxers are big, powerful, and fast. They are also quite safe and once you get the hang of one, you'll be in complete control. Work with cord and outlet behind you. Loop the cord over your working shoulder and release more yardage as you need it.

° Don't machine wax the floor right next to the wall or you'll scratch the paint. Do this small area by hand the first time. After that, ignore it for a few years. It won't get dirty and the wax won't wear off.

° Follow this step-by-step guide.

1: Attach a steel-wool disk to the machine and use it to loosen dirt and old wax.

2: Vacuum debris.

3: Put a new steel-wool disk on the machine and apply a small handful of wax directly to the steel wool, not the floor. (Never put wax directly onto the floor. When you move the machine over it, the fast circular motion of the disk will splatter it across your walls.) Turn the machine on. As you work, you will be able to see the wax on the floor. When it starts to thin out, apply more to the steel-wool disk. Don't try to put down an extra thick coat; it will not buff well. For extra protection, apply one thin coat, buff and apply another. Replace steel wool when it gets clogged with the wax.

4: Let wax dry for the time indicated by the manufacturer.

5: Buff with buffing pads.

To maintain a shine between waxing, buff with a small home electric waxer. When you can no longer work up a gleam, it's time to rewax. A liquid solvent wax, such as Preen, applied to heavy traffic areas between paste waxings, will prolong a shine. Don't attempt to use one of these products instead of paste wax. Applying one is time-consuming and difficult, and they don't buff to a hard enough finish.

If applying paste wax is more of a chore than you care to undertake, use one of the self-polishing floor waxes meant for wood floors, such as Johnson's Klear. These are not as easy to apply as liquid polishes meant for resilient flooring, and they are not very long-lasting, but they require much less effort than paste wax. Use a long-handled wax applicator (not a sponge mop) to apply and follow label directions. Don't use one of these products as a touch up between paste waxings. The formulas are not compatible.

Although we've said this before, it bears repeating. The biggest problem with maintaining a wood floor is repairing the damage done when grit is walked into its surface. This scratches and wears away the finish. So does the constant scraping of chair legs. Put floor guards on furniture and keep two doormats at each entryway, one on the outside, the other inside the door. Consider a "no-street-shoes-in-the-house" rule as well. In combination, these postpone the need for waxing and almost guarantee that the finish will stay intact. Always sweep or vacuum dust when it appears, especially in walkways, and under scatter rugs and doormats.

Wood Furniture
The key to success with wood furniture is restraint. Don't go overboard when applying polish, and ignore advertisements that imply that a polishing agent should be used every time you dust. It's true that furniture polishes offer some protection to

wood and have cleaning properties, but a little goes along way. Too much polish obscures the grain and turns murky on the surface. Some experts suggest that once a year is often enough to apply polish, others suggest that the job be done two or three times a year. It depends on how much wear the furniture receives. In other words, the dining table requires more frequent attention than the desk in the guest room. To maintain a gleam between application, rub briskly with a *fresh* soft cloth, after dusting. A bit of cool water on a rag will often remove soil without removing wax, or use a dab of your regular polish. Much modern furniture does not need the protection of polish at all. The finish is long lasting and treated to be resistant to water, alcohol, and heat. When this is the case, applying wax is purely a cosmetic gesture.

Which polish you use depends on the finish and your personal taste. There is no single best polish. Quality products (purchased from cabinetmakers and woodcraft shops) should be used when dealing with fine furniture or antiques. These are expensive, however, and unnecessary for ordinary pieces.

A paste wax, such as Butcher's Wax, offers good protection and a fairly long-lasting sheen, *but* it takes a lot of effort to apply and gives a very glossy shine that is not suitable to all finishes and is not always absorbed into a varnished surface. To obtain a slightly softer shine with less effort, use a liquid, such as Pride. Aerosols, such as Pledge (also available with a pump dispenser), deliver quick results that are especially suitable for glossy varnishes. These products, however, tend to build up quickly, *so don't use them too often* A cream wax (such as Johnson's Cream Polish) will maintain a low-luster finish.

Wood that has an oil finish should be cared for with an oil polish (such as lemon oil). This will not guard against staining or scratching, but it helps to keep oil-finished surfaces from drying out and has cleaning properties. Because it imparts a pleasing soft gleam with less effort than a wax-based polish, many people use one as an all-purpose polish. Never apply an oil polish to a waxed surface, or wax to an oiled surface. The two are incompatible. Before changing over from one to the other, it is necessary to remove the old polish (see remedial measures below). Dust oil-polished pieces frequently to keep them looking their best, as oil attracts and holds dust more readily than a waxed surface.

Whatever polish you decide to use, apply

it sparingly and wipe off as much as you can. You will be removing dirt as well as working up a shine, so replace your polishing rags frequently. All wood polishes are flammable and toxic. Fumes should not be breathed casually. Work with a window open.

Remedial Measures

To remove polish buildup or to prepare a wood surface so you can switch from an oil-based polish to wax (or the other way around), pour mineral spirits onto a clean soft rag and rub into surface using small circular motions. Do a small area at a time and change the rag when it shows soil. Work until the rag stays clean. Mineral spirits are toxic, flammable, and not meant for breathing!

To remove stains from oil-finished woods, use very fine steel wool dipped into mineral oil; rub lightly, following the grain of the wood. Use dry-cleaning fluid on oil-based stains, such as gravy, instead of mineral oil.

There are several tactics for repairing damage to a nonoil finish, such as varnish. White rings sometimes respond to a paste made from mineral oil and cigarette ashes. Rub this into the wood with your fingers. The only solution to black rings is refinishing. White haze is caused by heat or by applying wax over a damp finish. A new coat or two of polish may make this disappear. If not, remove the polish and start anew.

Scratches on a nonoil finish can sometimes be obscured by an application of your regular polish. You can also try colorless shoe polish. For deeper scratches, there are crayonlike sticks available at houseware stores that match the color of common wood finishes. Test to be sure that the match is good enough. These sticks impart a high gloss that may not be suitable for the existing finish. Old carpenter's trick: If you can find a wax shoe polish that closely approximates the color of your wood, apply it to the scratch with a cotton swab and buff. Shoe polish is less glossy than the crayon products.

The best measure is prevention before the fact. Protect your tabletops with coasters and heat-resistant pads; have good-sized ashtrays. In my opinion, dining and coffee tops are best protected by a barlike finish. It takes careful effort to apply, and is a bit repetitive, but once done it will look elegant for years.

The technique: Thoroughly sand the surface, finishing with fine sandpaper. Vacuum residue away. Brush on a thin coat of satin-finish polyurethane. Wait at least 24 hours. Lightly sand the surface with a fine grade of sandpaper. Again, vacuum residue away. Brush on a thin coat of satin-finish polyurethane. Wait at least 24 hours. Lightly sand the surface with a fine grade of sandpaper. Vacuum residue away. Brush on a thin coat of satin-finish polyurethane. Wait at least 24 hours. Apply a coat of paste wax, polishing to a hard, bright shine. Wax once a year, no more!

Warning note: The silicones contained in products like Pledge build up on surfaces and are not removed by ordinary refinishing efforts. Although the silicones are invisible to the naked eye, they cause pits to form on a new finish. If you've been using such a product, consult with an expert on wood care *before* refinishing. There are methods to remove a silicone buildup.

Warning note 2: Polyurethane fumes are really not good for you. If you have a protective mask, this is a time to use it.

Butcher Block

Butcher block that is used as a good preparation surface should not have a permanent finish. Varnish chips under the knife; the surface looks ugly and bits of varnish find their way into food. Purchase your butcher block untreated and apply mineral oil, which is nontoxic and doesn't turn rancid. Clean the surface with a mild detergent solution. Rinse and dry thoroughly. Sand lightly with a fine grade paper and vacuum away the residue. Apply mineral oil generously, rubbing it in with circular motions and fine steel wool. Let the oil remain on for 15 minutes; polish off the excess with a soft rag. Maintain with diluted dishwashing liquid and towel dry after washing. Do not cut raw meat, chicken, or fish on butcher block without disinfecting it afterwards (see page 108). When the surface starts to look dry and faded or becomes stained, sand and oil again.

Butcher block is sometimes used to top a dining table or dining counter. As a general rule, oil finishes do not offer adequate protection from spills, which can show up badly on light woods. Wine is a major offender. Consider applying the bar finish just described.

Wood Paneling Smooth wood and plywood surfaces usually have a tough protective finish with built-in gloss. They need no special protection. Dust as needed; spot clean and wash with a damp rag and Gentle Detergent Mix. Use Murphy Oil Soap for serious soil. If more care seems necessary, hesitate before applying wax. It's quite a job when a large area is involved. Liquid Gold can be used, but only after reading the label to make sure that it is safe for your particular surface. This product is damaging to some finishes. Lemon oil is another possibility. To apply either Liquid Gold or lemon oil to a wall (or kitchen cabinets), use long-handled floor wax applicator. A paint roller tray or oblong baking pan is easier to work from than a bucket. Do a section at a time and polish dry with a soft, clean rag. Replace the rag as needed. *Work with adequate ventilation.* Avoid using abrasives or steel wool.

Dust rough-textured paneling with a feather duster and vacuum occasionally. There is no successful method to wet clean or polish rough-textured wood. Fortunately, the texture disguises soil.

Ten

Maintaining A Bathroom

Soap and water, dominant features in any bathroom, dissolve dirt and spread it around. Let the water dry and you've got a cleaning problem. Wipe it up when it's still wet and the dirt comes right along with it. Take full advantage of this and clean as you go.

Keep cleaning gear hidden but accessible in the bathroom. Tuck a toilet brush behind the toilet to be used as needed. Place a squeeze bottle of dishwashing liquid next to the tub and add a little to bath water, or spray some into the bottom of the shower, before you turn on the water. This helps to prevent bathtub ring and to keep the bottom of the shower clean.

Make space in the medicine chest for a stack of folded paper towels, a small spray bottle of Ammonia Mix, and a sponge. When mirror, sink, and commode are steamy, wipe them dry with paper towels. If more cleaning seems called for, spray first with Ammonia Mix; wipe with a damp sponge. Unless you especially enjoy bathroom sparkle, this doesn't need to be done too often.

Every second or third week a more thorough cleaning may be called for. This depends on house standards and how faithful you've been to a wiping up routine. Lysol Bathroom Sink, Tub and Tile Cleaner is a nonabrasive product with disinfectant properties, which can be used on all bathroom surfaces including colored tiles (but excepting mirrors). A two-sided sponge (one side sponge, the other rough plastic) makes short work of bathtub ring, especially if you let your cleaning agent sit a few minutes. Use a brush to clean inside the toilet and don't forget the area right under the rim where the water comes out. Now and then clean behind the toilet and the side towards the wall, as well as the hidden parts of the floor. This usually means getting down on your hands and knees with a rag or sponge. While you're there, it's pretty easy to finish washing the floor, getting into corners where the mop doesn't reach.

There is no urgent need to sweep or vacuum a bathroom floor, but this should always be done before the floor is washed. It's simpler to sweep a small floor than to vacuum it. Wash the floor when necessary, the same way you would any other floor.

Meantime, place a large absorbent scatter rug in front of the tub, and perhaps the sink, if the room is large.

Very occasionally (twice a year is usually plenty), budget time for a big cleaning. Sort through the medicine chest and discard anything that's no longer wanted. Wash the shelves and get into cracks and runners with a butter knife wrapped in paper towel. Pour water into soap dishes and toothbrush holders to dissolve soap and toothpaste accumulations, and let sit for 10 minutes or so; scrub with the rough side of your two-sided sponge. To remove soap deposits and mildew stains from the shower walls, spray with Lysol Bathroom Cleaner, wipe down with a damp sponge mop, and rinse. Dry with a terry towel that's ready for the wash. For heavy accumulations, seek out Tile 'n Grout Magic, available in hardware stores, an aerosol product that lives up to the claims on its label.

To clean a bathroom wall, turn on the shower and let steam accumulate. Then, wipe down walls and ceilings with a damp sponge mop (no cleaning agent necessary). Wrap a towel around the mop to wipe the walls dry.

Mineral deposits and stains can present a special problem in areas where water is hard. Usually, a weekly application of scouring powder and a brisk scrub with a toilet brush will prevent toilet bowl discoloration. When this is not sufficient, purchase a toilet bowl cleanser designed to handle such staining. Follow all product directions, and store the cleanser well away from kids. Stains in sinks and tubs are easily prevented. If dripping water is the problem, place a sponge under the drip until the faucet can be repaired. Don't use scouring powder or toilet bowl cleaner to remove stains from sinks or tubs (see page 238). Try Zud or ask a hardware store clerk for the correct product. Stubborn white mineral deposits on shower stalls can usually be removed with Lime Off, a product sold in supermarkets.

Eleven

Coping

WHEN THERE'S NO TIME

For all of us, there are periods when other matters take precedence over housecare. This presents no great problem for the short term. However, if there's a long period of neglect – when one partner is holding down two jobs while the other is studying for exams and the baby is learning to walk, for example – special measures are in order.

Usually nutritional concerns are top priority. Stock up the freezer and pantry with easily prepared, healthful food staples. Concentrate on ingredients for one-dish meals and finger foods. If you can manage a cooking day or two, prepare such basics as rice, tomato sauce, soups, and casseroles and freeze them in small batches. Lay in a good supply of disposable aids such as paper plates, napkins, and towels, as well as aluminum foil, which can take the place of any number of pots. Have an inventory of nonperishable necessities on hand. The fewer soaps, condiments, light bulbs, toilet paper, etc., you need to purchase on a supermarket run, the sooner you'll get out of the store. Resolve to keep kitchen work surfaces clean and don't let dishes accumulate. Try to damp mop the floor once a week.

Laundry comes next. Apartment dwellers might do well to find a service laundromat that folds, and plan to drop off sheets, towels, and underwear once a week. Do what you can to keep laundry from piling up. Those who have their own machines might consider doing one wash a night, while preparing dinner or watching TV, to avoid a bigger job later. Others might do easily washed, no-iron garments when they take them off and let them drip-dry over the shower rod. Try to budget for some professional laundry or extra dry-cleaning.

The bathroom is simple. Place cleaning aids near the sink so they are accessible and inform housemates that their cooperation will be appreciated. Count out a week's supply of towels plus a few extras and hide the rest if your housemates tend to be wasteful in their use of towels.

Schedule at least one weekly vacuuming and dusting. Failing this, attend to heavy traffic areas. If you are truly pressed, consult Chapter Two for the preventive measures described there. Be especially careful to protect light-colored upholstered furniture and carpets.

At least once a week get rid of trash, old newspapers, magazines, and the like. If picking up is not your forte, establish cache pots and stacking spots so that objects won't be mislaid. Think in terms of categories, *i.e.,* pile reading matter in one place, delegate one spot for important messages and another for bills; be sure there's a big box for all *their* junk.

Consider having someone come to clean; as little as once a month will help. A helpful outside hand cleaning the kitchen or vacuuming the carpets is better than no help at all.

WHEN THINGS HAVE GONE TOO FAR

Many a time the following digging-out routine has stood me in good stead. It's also the first step in coming to terms with a chronic inability to deal with housework. When done, things will not be perfect by a long shot, but basic systems will be operable, so you can start to enjoy your home once more.

Preparation: It's best to schedule this for a long holiday weekend. Three to four days may be needed. Make sure that all necessary cleaning gear is in stock, including a good supply of paper towels, a fresh package of large plastic trash bags, and a large cardboard box for each house member, plus one extra. Have the makings for sandwiches or other convenience foods, and include orange or grapefruit juice, which are effective energy boosters. If you're weak on technique and want to do things right, look over the cleaning section of this book for how-tos. If a big job like paste waxing a floor or shampooing a carpet is on the agenda, arrange to have special equipment available.

When weather allows, keep windows open as you work. This helps to keep you alert.

Step 1: Straighten up a corner of one room, such as your bedroom. See that it is orderly and clean enough so that it can serve as a restful retreat.

Step 2: Move through the house with a garbage bag and collect as much "throw-away" as possible. Pitch out whatever is spoiled or questionable in the refrigerator including nearly empty jars. Get rid of broken toys, dry ball-point pens, out-dated medicines, squeezed-out tubes, scraps of soap, unread literature, clothing that is no longer serviceable or appealing. When in doubt, throw it away. Houses with fewer possessions are *always* easier to maintain. Besides, the more you can get rid of now, the less you will have to clean, or put away! Dispose of trash bags as they fill up.

Step 3: Again with trash bags, collect everything that needs to be laundered or dry-cleaned, including sheets, socks under the bed, towels, scatter rugs, pot holders, whatever. Put articles for the dry cleaner into one bag, things that require hand washing into another, things that can be simply tossed into a washing machine into still another. Separate dark objects from light in the washing machine bag and make sure that no special-care items have slipped in by istake. Ideally, carry this bag to a laundromat that will wash and fold. Because these establishments tend to operate in a somewhat haphazard fashion, you might want to follow the guidelines on page 183. Take cleaning to the dry cleaners and if you can swing the extra expense, include any hand washables that can be safely dry-cleaned or things that require pressing. What is left can be put to one side to be dealt with later.

Step 4: Concentrate on items that are out of place. (A cardboard box, used as a carrier, saves steps.) Carry objects to the room in which they belong and leave them there until everything has been collected. Then, put things away one room at a time. Keep a garbage bag handy, in case it's easier to dispose of something than to find a home for it. If you can't decide what to do with an article, and don't especially need it, put it into a big box and have such a box for each housemate. This is not the time for a major organizational effort but as you work, reorganize closets and drawers so that important items are easiest to reach. Make space in the back of the closet or in a lower drawer for infrequently used items or add them to the box of things that you don't know what to do with. Hide your own box for later organization; turn everybody else's over to them and let them make their own decisions.

Step 5: Dust and vacuum each room. Lift things like couch cushions and the edges of rugs; get under the bed and behind the couch. Don't forget picture frames, radiators, window sills, and the like.

Step 6: Clean and/or polish furniture; spiff up knickknacks, include mirrors and picture glass.

Step 7: Damp mop floors, leaving kitchen and bathroom floors for later.

Step 8: Clean the bathroom, including fixtures, medicine chest, mirrors, and floors. Wash out the toothbrush holders. Clean under the sink and behind the toilet. Ignore bathroom walls and shower stalls for the time being.

Step 9: Next comes the kitchen. If the freezer is iced up or the oven smokes, include these in your cleanup. Otherwise, concentrate on visible surfaces such as counter tops, small appliances, the fronts and tops of the stove and refrigerator; clean the inside of the refrigerator as well. Do the floor last.

Step 10: Finally, do any major job that makes a significant difference in the appearance or operating capacity of the home. This depends strictly on what you care about. If clean windows, a waxed floor, a shampooed rug, or a washed kitchen or bathroom wall are important to you at this point, then the job is worth doing. Finish up with hand laundry and ironing.

Upkeep: You've just been through a major effort. You now have the option of keeping it up regularly on a small scale or coasting along until the next big clean.

Finally: Homecare is only a small part of life. It's certainly a meaningful part and when attended to, it makes life considerably more pleasant. However, other concerns often take precedence. Do the best you can with the time and energy that you have to give. Don't worry about the rest. The jobs will still be there next week (or next year) when you are better able to attend to them.

Your home is as close to a castle as you are ever likely to get. The right to decide what needs doing – and when and how it will be done – goes with the domain.

Bibliography

Reluctant though I may be to admit it, *Home Free* does not offer a solution to every problem that a householder may encounter. The following most useful references expand upon the different aspects of homecare. A few might be valuable additions to your library. Paperback editions are so described.

HOUSEWORK

Ager, Stanley, and Fiona St. Aubyn. *The Butler's Guide to Clothes Care, Managing the Table, Running the Home and Other Graces.* New York: Simon and Schuster/ Fireside Edition, 1981. (Paperback) This delightful book manages to be both elegant in tone and homey. It's also surprisingly practical. Of special interest: sections on clothing care; polishing metals; waxing furniture. (A hardcover edition was published under the title *Ager's Way to Easy Elegance.* Indianapolis: Bobbs-Merrill Co., Inc., 1980.)

Conran, Shirley. *Superwoman.* New York:

Crown Publishers, 1978 (Paperback: new York: Bantam Books, Inc., 1979.) Those having difficulty shaking off guilty feelings about the quality of their housework will find this book useful.

Habeeb, Virginia T. *The Ladies' Home Journal Art of Homemaking*. New York: Simon and Schuster, 1973. (Paperback) In 588 pages, this book covers a lot of ground, incorporating much of the research done by home economic specialists at colleges and universities around the country. It is an excellent manual for home-owners as it discusses such things as kitchen design and large appliances. Well indexed.

Libien, Lois, and Margaret Strong. *Super Economy Housecleaning*. New York: William Morrow and Company Inc., 1976. This book reflects both independent thinking and conscientious research, in a no-nonsense approach geared for speed. Well indexed.

Moore, Alma Chestnut. *How to Clean Everything*. New York: Simon and Schuster, 1952, 1960, 1968, 1977. (Paperback) A how-to compendium that is broken down by type of material and surface. Useful discussions of cleaning chemicals and how they work.

Not a manual, but a very helpful back-up reference.

ORGANIZATION

McCullough, Bonnie Runyan. *Bonnie's Household Organizer*. New York: St. Martin's Press, 1980. (Paperback) Geared to families, with useful tips for getting children and housemates to take a full share of household responsibility.

Winston Stephanie. *Getting Organized*. New York: W. W. Norton, 1978. (Paperback: Warner Books, 1979.) As I said in the text, this book has quickly become a classic in a crowded field. At least half of its contents pertains to establishing (and maintaining) household order.

CULINARY MATTERS

Brody, Jane E. *Jane Brody's Nutrition Book*. New York: W. W. Norton, 1981. (Paperback: Bantam Books Inc., 1982.) This book, which represents a major effort by a knowledgeable health and science writer, imparts much clarity to the confused subject of modern nutrition. Included are guidelines for incorporating weight loss into the daily diet as well as commonsense suggestions for feeding a family.

Burros, Marian. *Keep It Simple*. New York: William Morrow Co., 1981. A cookbook for those who enjoy good food but don't have time to prepare it. Based on sound nutritional principles.

INTERIOR DECORATING

Conran, Terence. *The House Book*. New York: Crown Publishers, 1976.

—. *The Kitchen Book*. New York: Crown Publishers, 1977. (Both titles are also offered as paperbacks by Crown Publishers.) At first glance these handsome illustrated books appear to be only for those who wish to redecorate or reequip their homes. They are much more practical than they appear, incorporating tips for kitchen use, cleaning, and the workings of appliances, large and small, as well as other useful hints. They also discuss the care requirements of commonly used materials, including flooring, wall coverings, work and furniture surfaces, carpeting, along with extensive lists of manufacturers and suppliers. *The House Book* contains a good section on kitchens, although *The Kitchen Book* is much more complete.

HOME REPAIR AND RELATED TOPICS

Curry, Barbra. *Okay, I'll Do It Myself: A Handy Woman's Primer.* New York: Harcourt Brace & World, 1962. Clear, readable instructions for basic home repairs and improvements.

Reader's Digest Complete Do-It-Yourself Manual. New York, 1973.

Schuler, Stanley, and Elizabeth Meriwether Schuler. *The Householder's Encyclopedia.* New York: Galahad Books, 1973. Repairs and *everything* else from minimal cleaning tactics to how to brighten aluminum storm windows to how to choose and sharpen a knife. Well organized and concise.

OF MISCELLANEOUS INTEREST

Center for Science in the Public Interest. *The Household Pollutants Guide.* Garden City, N.Y.: Anchor Press/Doubleday, 1978. (Paperback) About dangerous cleaning (and other) household chemicals. Guidelines for use and effective substitutes.

Kesselman-Turkel, Judi, and Franklynn Peterson. *The Homeowner's Book of Lists.* Chicago: Contemporary Books, Inc., 1982. (Paperback) Useful information, ranging from a consumer information directory to standard bed linen sizes to interest rates on loans. Handy!

OTHER SOURCES OF INFORMATION

Consumer Reports, a monthly magazine published by the Consumer Union. (For information: Subscription Director Consumer Reports Box 111, Mount Vernon, N.Y. 10550.) This publication is produced with great integrity by a nonprofit watchdog group that does independent research on matters of household interest. The emphasis is on safety, efficiency, and cost; the avowed purpose, "to initiate and to cooperate with individual and group efforts seeking to create and maintain decent living standards." A resource!

Better Homes and Gardens, Family Circle, Ladies' Home Journal, McCalls, Redbook, Woman's Day, and the like are another valuable source of information. With the exception of *Good Housekeeping and Better Homes and Gardens,* which sometimes briefly discuss housework, these magazines tend to ignore the mechanics of day-to-day maintenance, although they offer many household tips. They consistently give good information on meal planning, developments in nutrition, storage devices, new appliances and decorating (including how-to instructions for building space-saving furniture or designing a workable home office or child's room). Each of these very practical magazines is editorially slanted to a somewhat different audience, defined by income level and degree of sophistication. But for the past several years, all of them have given major attention to the needs of the working homemaker. Despite the female orientation, any man seriously interested in household matters would do well to investigate these magazines. The information they impart is not easily obtained elsewhere.

The food and home sections of newspapers, especially in big cities, are another source of information, and home repair columns are yet another, which often stress correct maintenance techniques so that problems can be avoided in the future.